In loving memory of my parents, Victor Hugo and Amada Maria. Your love, sacrifice, wisdom, and work ethic have been the guiding light in my life. Your attributes shaped my leadership frame and mental model. Though you are no longer with me, your spirits live on in every page of this book.

SAFE

CULTIVATING ENGAGEMENT
ONE LEADER AT A TIME

ZONE

DR. MARIA SILVA-PALACIOS

The Safe Zone: Cultivating Engagement One Leader at a Time
Copyright © 2024 Dr. Maria Silva-Palacios

Published by Ergon Culture Solutions

Paperback ISBN: 979-8-9902258-0-0
Hardcover ISBN: 979-8-9902258-1-7
E-book ISBN: 979-8-9902258-2-4
Library of Congress Control Number: 2024906730

Although the author and publisher have made every effort to ensure that the information in this book was correct at press time, the author and publisher do not assume and hereby disclaim any liability to any party for any loss, damage, or disruption caused by errors or omissions. Some names and identifying details have been changed to protect the privacy of individuals.

Printed in the United States

"Dr. Silva-Palacios' first-person, firsthand narrative stands out in books on leadership. It offers profound, immediate, and authoritative insights, making it enjoyable to read and prompting readers to reflect on their own leadership styles and values. Although the book is specifically about leadership in the utilities sector, Dr. Silva-Palacios' observations and principles of leadership are universal and apply to leaders in all fields."

—**Dr. Steven Simon**, President, Culture Change Consultants, Inc.

"Dr. Maria believes in one of the crucial authentic leadership principles—that in order to transform themselves and their organizations, leaders need to practice self-awareness, self-reflection and self-management. Through the real stories in her book about safety culture and leadership, she is calling on organizational leaders to make the changes needed to keep their people safe."

—**Dr. Yasmin Davidds**, Founder & CEO, Dr. Yasmin Davidds
Leadership Institute

"Dr. Maria extends a virtual hand to the reader to bring them along like a friend on a hike. From her Ecuadorian roots to working side-by-side with CEOs and frontline crews, she makes us feel like she is there with us, in the room. As we synchronize with her stories and experience, her book releases a higher level of thought within ourselves for a better understanding of how to 'Cultivate Engagement One Leader at a Time.' This book will increase your bandwidth of ideas for moving forward in your Safe Zone."

—**William N. Martin**, CEO/President, Think Tank Project LLC, CUSP, RN,
NRP, DIMM, Speaker, Writer, Change Agent, Pattern Disruptor,
Myth Buster, and Translator

"An insightful guide for leaders, this remarkable book delves into the crucial aspects of setting the tone within an organization. With a focus on authentic leadership and fostering meaningful relationships with employees, it offers invaluable wisdom and practical strategies to create a positive and engaging work environment. A must-read for aspiring and seasoned leaders alike!"

—**Rodney Karr**, Vice President, Leadership, Safety, and Training, MasTec West

"Maria has exposed the inner self we have as we go through life challenges and learnings. She succinctly identifies for the reader everyday encounters that help us understand how to possibly deal with these encounters in a healthy, productive manner. This book provides the tools to understand and overcome our initial reactions to tough situations and become a more positive person in life and work. Maria defines for the reader the reality of working in a predominantly male environment, and she provides guidance as to best maneuver through the machismo testosterone-driven work force. She helps the reader with the understanding ability to create change with a partnership attitude, making the receivers of change become cheerleaders for improvement. With her knowledge and experience, she takes the reader from her personal experiences through life, along with her work encounters, so that the reader can relate and emerge as a successful person throughout what life may bring."

—**Steve Brown**, Retired Safety Director, Safety Par Electric

"Maria is able to share some firsthand insights from her experience in working with electrical trade workers. These insights are the key to helping to understand the culture and, more importantly, the things that influence this culture. This book also provides very actionable approaches that, if effectively implemented, significantly improve the readiness of workers with a goal of reducing the probability of soft tissue injuries."

—**Andrew Martinez**, Retired Utility Industry Vice President of Safety

"Maria tells a passionate story of her personal journey through employee interviews and real-world experiences working her way up from a personal trainer to a full-time safety leader in one of the country's largest utility companies. Maria's experiences have led her to write this book outlining what it takes for a company leader to become better engaged with his/her workforce to be a true safety influencer."

—**Salvatore Caccavale**, Corporate Director, Environmental, Safety, and Security, Martz Bus

"Maria is a consummate safety professional, and her insights will cause you to think differently about how you approach the workplace as a leader. *The Safe Zone* is filled with real-life examples that serve as a powerful reminder of how influential leaders are when it comes to influencing—and ultimately changing—the safety culture."

—**Christine Fanous**, Utility Industry Director

CONTENTS

FOREWORD

One of the best benefits of participating as a speaker at a national safety event is the networking you are able to experience with other speakers who are attending and presenting as well. That is how I came to meet "Dr. Maria" in a chance encounter as we each prepared for our individual sessions. While you may think it is easy to stand up in front of safety professionals and share your message, the truth is it takes many hours of preparation, an ability to overcome anxiety, and fortitude to accomplish this. Many of us will review and practice our presentations right up to the minute we deliver them in front of our audience. This is where Dr. Maria and I made our introductions, exchanged contact information, and discussed safety and how we both approach our audience in these settings.

Our conversation that day was enlightening, not only around safety but around the connections we already had related specifically to the electrical and utility industry we all benefit from. As she is the wife of a local IBEW representative in California, we immediately had a connection since I am an IBEW inside electrician and have been a member for over forty years. Maria explained she had conducted research and written her dissertation on the physical activities of utility line workers. It is these line workers who answer the call after each emergency to restore power, provide lights and communications to our nation, and allow us to return to normal activities.

As the son of a lineman, I know how grueling utility line work is and the toll it takes on the body. There are long hours of physical labor, heavy equipment and tools used by line workers, and the extensive reaching many tasks demand—since working with energized electrical circuits and conductors must be performed using insulated tools or "hot sticks" at a distance to protect from electrical shock. Many utility workers find that by the time they reach the age of forty, forty-five at the latest, their bodies are spent, and it is difficult to continue to work safely and effectively in the trade they have chosen.

I have a daughter who is a mechanical engineer, and when she started, she shared some of the challenges she experienced as a female in an environment that was dominated by male workers. The utility field is very similar to this by having a very masculine dominance over the years. For Dr. Maria to influence these workers, she had to use varying styles of communication and build a level of trust with all the workers so that they would open up and listen clearly to the suggestions and benefits of her experience and degree in the field of kinesiology, that is, the study of the body's movements to help individuals improve their mobility and quality of life.

Through her efforts, she was able to influence the companies and workers and show how simple changes in routine, dedicated exercises, and safety culture can bring a huge return on investment for everyone, personally and professionally. Maria specialized in identifying body movements that can cause pain and injury and, through research, helped to identify some exercises that improve core functions and allow these workers to live long and productive lives performing their trade. Understanding ergonomic issues and the unique positioning and stresses of the utility worker allowed her to really delve deep into the answers she received from the line workers she interviewed as part of this endeavor.

One of the major benefits of her book is that it helps to identify core leadership values that every worker, supervisor, and company should embrace if they are to have an impact on fellow workers in the field. Whether you're supervising directly or leading the work from an upper-level position within the organization, your actions have the greatest influence on those around you. If you take a shortcut or put less emphasis on safety, that philosophy will trickle down to the whole crew. However, if you participate in and lead the discussion and emphasize the importance and benefits of safety, including warming up the body for the day's activities, you will see the difference you make in other people's lives.

By reflecting on the leaders in her life and showing that compassion, empathy, and commitment, both personal and professional, are the key tenets of an authentic leader, we can all learn to explore these traits in ourselves from her examples. Hearing the stories from the workers about their foremen and supervisors who had the most influence on their crews gives clear evidence of the benefits of being an authentic leader. We all learn through experience, whether it is our own experience or the experience of others. When we can share our experiences to help others and prepare them for their roles in leadership and life, we can all be influencers to ensure we preserve our most important resources—our friends, family, and coworkers.

Since that chance encounter, I have had the opportunity to invite Dr. Maria to participate in our industry safety events and share her knowledge and research with our association member attendees, in addition to attending some of her presentations at other conferences. Her sessions are well attended, and the audience is able to relate to her message about safety and leadership and making a difference from that day forward.

—**Wesley L. Wheeler**, SMS, CESCP, NECA Executive Director of Safety, IBEW Inside Journeyman Wireman Electrician since 1984

INTRODUCTION

n the editor's note for Bill George's 2007 book *True North: Discover your Authentic Leadership*, renowned author, American scholar, organizational consultant, and leadership studies guru Warren Bennis wrote that his hope and goal was to "spark new intellectual capital by sharing ideas positioned at an angle to conventional thought—in short, to publish books that disturb the present in the service of a better future."[1]

One of the central tenets of Bill George's *True North* is to "know thyself." Mr. George asserts that, as leaders, we must know, understand, and embrace who we are, including our assets and flaws equally, and then deal with them directly. Another tenet is that the journey to knowing ourselves must include our life stories, including our crucibles. Crucibles are life experiences that are often traumatic and serve as catalysts for self-actualization.

> To "know thyself" is not an easy deed. It's a process that requires daily and sometimes hourly intentional introspection, self-reflection, and insight—and this process takes courage.

---

[1] Bill George, *True North: Discover Your Authentic Leadership* (San Francisco, CA: Jossey-Bass/John Wiley & Sons, 2007).

As I began to write this book, Mr. Bennis's words resonated with me deeply. I thought about the company and organization where I worked and our mutual struggle in our commitment to responsible change.

To "know thyself" is not an easy deed. It's a process that requires daily and sometimes hourly *intentional* introspection, self-reflection, and insight—and this process takes courage. What I've learned in my educational and leadership journey is that to transform organizations and "disturb the present in the service of a better future," we need to be *courageous leaders*; however, I never considered myself as one. Instead, and before my in-depth studies about leadership, I considered myself an "intuitive leader," meaning that I followed my inner voice or "gut," as we refer to it often. Following my gut-leadership style worked for me for the most part because, instinctively, I was an employee-centric leader. That is until I began to understand and connect how my life story directly influenced my leadership style. I share my leadership genesis in subsequent chapters; however, in the spirit of authenticity and transparency, I begin by sharing a glimpse of one of my most personal victories that has shaped my courageous leadership mindset in the last decade.

My family and I immigrated to the United States from Ecuador when I was six years old. Almost immediately upon arrival, my older brother, the now Dr. Victor Silva-Palacios, became a father figure to me and more so after our father passed away in 2005. Growing up, Victor was always extremely athletic and mastered several sports. Later in life, he became an avid triathlete. Because I, too, was athletic, he begged me (more like harassed me, as a big brother usually does) for *years* to participate in a triathlon with him. My response to him all of those years was a resounding *no*. Until 2011, for my birthday, when *he decided* it was time for me to take the plunge (pardon the pun) and join him in a 2012 triathlon. As a birthday gift, he gave me five swimming lessons with a private coach. Victor was aware I *did not* know how to swim and why, so it was a running joke that for me to learn how to swim, the swim coach would have to be a coach-slash-therapist.

I had a fear of water. Not any ol' run-of-the-mill fear; it was a paralyzing fear that I had not faced, let alone overcome. You see, as a little girl in Ecuador, I had been physically abused, and water was used as punishment. Victor tells me that in our neighborhood in Ecuador, everyone knew when I was being punished because they could hear my blood-curdling screams as I was dragged into the shower while my head was held under the shower head.

As far as I can remember, my relationship with water was a love-fear. On one hand, I experienced the ocean and pool water as soothing, peaceful, and refreshing. Yet, on the other hand, I was absolutely terrified of it, most of all in the shower. In fact, it wasn't until twenty-plus years ago (and with lots of therapy) that I was able to shower and allow the water to run over my face. I could only allow the water to run on the back of my head. As an adult now, my fear of water makes sense to me, but it didn't as a child. As a psychotherapist, Victor understood my reluctance to join him, yet he knew it was the right time for him to nudge me so that I could face my fear. He believed in me even though I didn't. He knew that I was courageous, I would conquer this fear, and I would claim my victory.

I took those five swimming lessons. The first one was absolute torture relived because I had to learn from beyond the basics. The swim coach guided me tenderly on how to blow bubbles while submerged—argh—however, I did it! I then moved on and joined my local YMCA for group and individual lessons. I had approximately four months to learn to swim eighteen laps, which seemed impossible then. I made it my mantra: eighteen laps, eighteen laps, eighteen laps (insert calming breath). Those months of swimming three times a week came and went far too quickly.

The day of the triathlon arrived, and I was nervous, terrified, and excited. Victor promised he would stay with me throughout the entire triathlon. I remember vividly looking up as I was coming up for air during my last lap to see Victor's face. He was smiling a huge Colgate smile while cheering me on that I was almost done (tears)!! Once I was out of the water, we ran quickly to the transition area to change into our bike gear. We champed that leg of the race, and then the last part was the run. Oh, what a feeling. Running was my sweet spot, so we ran almost effortlessly and crossed the finish line together—just as he had promised. We hugged as we both cried, feeling overwhelmed with joy for what I had just conquered with him by my side.

My next few triathlons were in the ocean. I figured: Go big or go home. The ocean triathlons triggered my trauma even more because of the tides, currents, and waves that caused the water to splash all over my face, and, oftentimes, I was submerged involuntarily. Still, I conquered them too. My other mantra became: "Just swim buoy to buoy." Much like the "know thyself" process I mentioned above, learning to swim was not an easy feat. It took commitment, tenacity, perseverance, and intentionality.

Flash-forward ten-plus years and seven ocean and pool triathlons later, and I have found peace and joy in the water. I did just as Warren Bennis asserted that leaders must do. I embraced my flaws (insert fears) and my assets (insert courage) and dealt with them directly (insert learning to swim) so I could "disturb my present in the service of a better future." My mantra of "just swim buoy to buoy" became a metaphor for facing *any* challenges I encountered, including obtaining my doctoral degree. My life story of learning to swim serves as a metaphor for my leadership and educational journey as well.

Above, I shared parts of *my story* with you. Why is this important, and what does this have to do with leadership? You see, to me, it has *everything* to do with leadership, and you will discover why in more detail in a later chapter. Until then, here is a sneak peek.

Our life experiences, both good and bad, shape the lens through which we see our lives and others as well. In a nutshell, it impacts how we lead.

We all have a story to share, and as leaders who want to transform people and organizations, acknowledging and embracing our life experiences is foundational. As Warren Bennis has said, "Becoming a leader is synonymous with becoming yourself. It is precisely that simple, and it is also that difficult."[2]

> Our life experiences, both good and bad, shape the lens through which we see our lives and others as well.

The stories in this book are from the qualitative research study I conducted for my doctoral dissertation at the University of Southern California. These are the stories of the utility linemen (or line gods, as many of them would refer to themselves) who participated in my study. They are transparent, candid, and vulnerable and are based solely on their perspectives and experiences, in their own words. My study's topic centered on employee engagement in organizational injury-prevention programs, and it's one that has been very near and dear to my heart for many years.

When I first started my career with this utility company, I had just completed my bachelor's degree in kinesiology. I was a personal trainer and group exercise instructor when I was hired as a "stretch-and-flex" coach by one of this utility's safety specialists. I started at one location. Back, knee, and shoulder sprains and strains were prevalent within the linemen workforce, so my job was to lead the linemen in preventative exercises and movements to address these affected areas. Before I knew it, I was traveling to several locations.

---

[2] Warren Bennis, from *Taking Charge: Lessons in Leadership* by David Wright (Insight Publishing, 2003).

The reviews I received were great, and eventually, one of the safety specialists referred me to the company's corporate fitness center manager, who was looking for an injury-prevention program coordinator, a group exercise instructor, and a trainer. I was interviewed shortly after the referral and hired on the spot. I dove in quickly and began to travel across the company's 50,000-square-mile radius, facilitating, along with other staff members, the program that the corporate fitness center had in place already.

Much like when I was a stretch-and-flex coach, some linemen were receptive and appreciated that their organization was providing this service for them, while others—not so much. I called them "cross arms" because, at first, they'd listen to me with crossed arms and an expression of "not me." (Also, in the electrical utility world, a crossarm is the four-by-four beam placed at the top of the pole to support the lines.) In this story, I'm using it as a metaphor for the person not wanting to listen. For me, both the stretch-and-flex and the injury-prevention program coordinator positions served as a great primer for what was to follow. I quickly learned the organization's culture dynamic. I'm grateful for these experiences because they helped me foster trusting relationships with employees and their leadership, which later was very useful for my career as a safety specialist in that same organization.

From the beginning of my career as the stretch-and-flex coach, I had a genuine desire to help the linemen prevent sprains and strains. I was intrigued by the linemen's lack of willingness to participate in these exercise movements aimed at reducing their sprain and strain injuries. Also, because I knew firsthand how a strain or sprain could affect their ability to perform regular daily tasks and alter their ability to work or enjoy their time off, I was baffled as to why they lacked interest in participating. I took it to heart that many did not want anything to do with the programs. Instead of personalizing their refusal to participate, I wanted to gain an understanding of the reason they refused, so I began to ask them questions about their why.

I received an array of responses. Some shared that they believed it was an intrusion of their personal space. Others *repeatedly* shared that they didn't trust the leadership when they espoused one moment that they wanted to keep them safe and in the next encouraged them to take "safety shortcuts" on the job or promoted a "hurry up" attitude. Since I didn't work in safety at that time, I didn't understand what they meant. Ten years later, however, I became a safety professional supporting this workforce, and it all began to make sense.

As a safety specialist in this organization, and because of my kinesiology background, I continued to play a critical role in preventing sprains and strains in the organizations I supported. I served as lead, co-lead, injury-prevention program facilitator, ergonomic subject-matter expert, and various other roles, all aimed at the prevention of these injuries. During my career as a safety specialist, three things remained the same: 1) Sprains and strains were always the leading injuries in this organization; 2) participation was always low regardless of the program provided; and 3) my fascination with "why" the low engagement deepened.

When I decided to pursue my doctoral degree, one of my mentors suggested that for my dissertation topic, I needed to choose something I was very passionate about. Naturally, I chose this topic about leadership's critical role in influencing and motivating their employees to engage in worksite injury-prevention programs.

Last year, I spoke at a safety conference where I had the opportunity to share my dissertation findings. I was feeling increasingly nervous and excited as more and more attendees filled the conference room, to the point of standing room only. After my session was over, I was approached by safety professionals, as well as a few utility linemen who served on the safety committees.

They expressed that my presentation resonated with them because their biggest challenges were exactly what I shared: *how to reduce the staggering number of sprain and strain injuries* causing pain and limited work for a large percentage of the workforce and costing companies millions of dollars and *how to increase employee engagement* in worksite injury-prevention programs designed to reduce these injuries.

> Leaders do have the power to influence if they commit to taking action and applying the attributes of authentic leadership.

I appreciated their concern and shared that I was writing a book about this. I mentioned to them that my hope is that the reader will take away how critical a leader's role is in setting the tone for their organization. Then, they will understand the importance of developing relationships with their employees based on trust that will result in both a physically and psychologically safe work environment.

Believe it or not, I've had conversations with leaders who have convinced themselves that they don't have *that* type of power—the power to influence others. I beg to differ. Leaders *do have* the power to influence *if* they commit to taking action and applying the attributes I discuss in the latter part of this book. After that, it's a domino effect. A safety culture *can and will* transform.

As one of my safety colleagues, William "Bill" Martin, shared with me during a recent conversation, "Team relationships affect team safety." I would add to Bill's quote: "And leader relationships with their team affect safety." In the coming chapters, we will look at this issue through the lens of the organizational obstacles and motivational factors I discovered in my research and then explore the influence of authentic leadership.

Along with the linemen's stories, I share anecdotes about my personal leadership journey as a safety professional. Much like parenting, being a leader does not come with a manual, and sometimes, it comes with bouts of paralyzing fear and doubt about whether we can lead and influence successfully. My hope and goal are that as you read each chapter, it will serve as an inspirational manual to uncover or rediscover your leadership style.

I encourage you to consider reflecting on your own personal life story and ask yourself, "How has my story shaped my leadership journey? What changes do I need to make to 'disturb my present' in the service of my employees' safety and transform my organization one step (or buoy) at a time?"

CHAPTER 1

CULTURE

I n 2022, I attended a safety conference, and I had the privilege of moderating a session titled "Safety from the C-Suite: Leading People Safely in Today's Business Environment," presented by a very well-known and highly respected CEO in the safety industry, Brian Fielkow. I felt unusually nervous. There I was, in the *largest* ballroom in that convention center. I'm talking about three HUGE screens (one center stage and two on each side of the stage)! There were high-tech video, lighting, and audio support people everywhere scurrying about to ensure everything was nothing short of perfection, a backstage meet area (that I officially named the "green room"), and a football-field-size stage (OK, so maybe not a football field, but it was *large*). I got there approximately twenty-five minutes prior and had a chance to chat with Mr. Fielkow, who was in the "green room" area prior to his presentation. I introduced myself; actually, I reintroduced myself because I had interviewed him at the same conference in Houston in

2018 for a school assignment. Just as he was in 2018, he was very pleasant and humble, so it eased my nerves.

During his presentation, Mr. Fielkow weaved in *many* poignant statements that I wanted to capture; however, my fingers couldn't write fast enough. He shared that to create a culture where both employees and the organization flourish, leadership must communicate the value of injury prevention from the C-level to the immediate supervisors. He said, "Safety is a core value, and perceptions matter," and "Belief drives behavior."

Everything he shared struck a chord with me, especially a few of his statements pertaining to organizational culture, which caused me to reflect on the interviews I conducted with the linemen:

"Production pressure creates risks."

"If safety is truly a value, then we shouldn't compromise it."

"We as leaders can influence what employees believe."

I realized as Mr. Fielkow was speaking that what he shared that day was personified by the linemen's own compelling experiences that they'd shared with me.

There is a reason why Mr. Fielkow was acknowledged as one of the CEOs Who "Get It" featured in February 2022's National Safety Council's *Safety+Health* magazine, a well-known publication that safety professionals and leaders subscribe to. In this issue, Mr. Fielkow shared his perspective and passion for keeping his employees safe through his personal safety journey. He shared that he understands how an organizational culture sets the tone for overall success, especially in the safety realm. He's adamant (an understatement) that "safety is not a department; it's a way of life," and his mindset is that leaders must walk the walk and talk the talk; otherwise, their employees will emulate their leaders' actions, not their words.

Everything Mr. Fielkow shared in his presentation that day confirmed my experience in my professional safety career and what I studied during my doctoral journey.

The essence of this chapter consists of the linemen's stories of their experiences, perceptions, and perspectives about the organization's culture of a heightened focus on rules and tools, prioritizing emergent work over safety, and the influence leaders' actions had on their employees. My hope is that the following linemen's stories resonate with you, just as Brian Fielkow's message did with me.

▌Rules and Tools Culture

The utility industry has a unique organizational culture. It is inherently compliance-based and must adhere to strict regulatory requirements; it is undeniable why it must be this way. The occupational hazards that exist in this industry can potentially be catastrophic and sometimes fatal. As my colleague Bill Martin says, however, "Safety compliance is not as crucial if the culture is right."

Early on in my career as a safety professional in this company, I didn't understand why there was such an emphasis on compliance; however, in a New York minute I understood clearly why it was not only important but critical. Throughout my career, I witnessed the safety organization grappling with finding the balance between the ability to adopt an integrated approach to safety that included cooperation—meaning buy-in, tone-from-the-top, and engagement at all levels—without sacrificing compliance. By the time I left the company, they were making strides but still had a long way to go. I also understood and still understand that it's about progress, not perfection.

During my interviews with the linemen, I was extremely pleased to hear the participants' acknowledgment of an organizational culture shift (for the better) over the last five years. They shared that it was fostered specifically at the highest leadership level to set the tone for all organizational leaders to emphasize all aspects of safety. This shift included the expectation for leadership of all levels to be more present and accessible for employee concerns regarding fatigue, driving safely, additional needed equipment, and safety resources to ensure employees returned home safely after work. When I asked the linemen about what their immediate supervisors did to create a culture of safety, a few of them described their immediate supervisors as being supportive of safety. Despite their acknowledgment of a culture shift, however, almost 80 percent of them shared that leadership focused primarily on strict enforcement of safety rule compliance rather than participation in the injury-prevention program.

When I interviewed lineman John, he described his immediate supervisor as someone who focused on fostering a culture of following and enforcing safety rules. He shared, "Other than enforcing the Accident Prevention Manual rules that we have at work and all the safety protocols and just making sure guys really do what they're supposed to do, that's it." Additionally, John shared with me that he had experienced a positive shift in the organizational safety culture from the executive leadership. He said, "From about five years to now, they've been really expressing safety. If you're tired, don't do this; safety is before work." John continued to share that he was unsure if his immediate supervisor was being supportive of safety *only* because it was mandated by the executive leadership level and because he was a union steward:

> *Because I'm a union steward, we get a lot of support from him when it comes to safety. I don't know if it is because he knows he's going to get some grievances or because that's where he sees safety. I'll say he's been very supportive when it comes to safety because it's been handed down from the top supervisors. Really, they're not pushing the boundaries when it comes to safety. If we need this and we need that, or if something breaks, we have their 100 percent support most of the time.*

Another lineman, Michael, shared a different perspective than John. He experienced it as "the organizational leaders' perspective on safety was to follow all the rules and do as you're told." In contrast to the organizational leaders, he said of his immediate supervisor, "He cares about safety. It's very rare that he, honestly, doesn't care about safety. I must give it to him; he is pretty safety conscious; I'd say 98 percent of the time."

Lineman Thomas' perspective was just like Michael's. He reported that his immediate supervisor "for the most part, has my back when it comes to safety." And about the executive leadership, he stated:

I feel that sometimes, when we have people in a power position that never came from the field, they don't understand these safety aspects of our job. They will push and sometimes forget and throw safety out the window. It's up to us and my immediate supervisor to squash that with our higher-ups. My immediate supervisor is the one who emphasized safety mostly as it pertained to performing job tasks. Safety is always a word that's iterated. Anytime we're talking about any task, really, it's on our tailboard (pre-job briefing) forms. Anytime we're working a big job, any type of weekend work or night outages, my immediate supervisor makes crew visits.

Thomas also shared that his immediate supervisor generally focuses on ensuring safety rules are followed, such as "checking certain safety items on his list, putting the chocks down in front or back of the tires so the truck doesn't roll away. Also, he makes sure we have our hard hats on, we're wearing our other PPE [personal protective equipment], leather gloves, and Nomex [fire resistant] suits."

Lineman William described that his immediate supervisor expects employees "to know the rules. We know we're supposed to follow the rules and work techniques." He added that the organization's leadership fosters a culture of enforcing rules and noted, "As far as our district leadership team, they tell you to follow the safety rules, but that's about it."

When I interviewed Henry, a lineman from another district, he shared that the executive leadership espoused the importance of following safety rules: "It's talked about quite often and definitely something that they've made a big deal and made it known that they're going to make a priority." Henry said his immediate supervisor reminds them constantly of the rules they need to consider and added, "I've been on jobs when I've heard him say, 'Hey, do this or change that.' Meaning, 'Add extra cones; hey, take extra cover-up.'" He recounted that on several occasions, his supervisor would bring up additional possible issues or hazards, asking the crews constantly, "Did you guys remember to think of this? Did you guys consider these two or three extra things?"

After Henry shared these examples of some of the leaders' focus on rules and tools, he mentioned an additional example in which his immediate supervisor is supportive of safety. He shared that his immediate supervisor makes himself available to the crews by "being present around the crew during actual crew work rather than just telling guys that if they need more help, more hands, assistance, more time, just let us know." This led Henry to believe that his immediate supervisor took an interest in his safety and that it wasn't only about following orders and rules.

Jack, a lineman from a different district than Henry, shared with me that his organizational leadership and his immediate supervisor prioritized safety rules *as well as* their personal safety. He noted,

> *In the organization, leaders take safety very seriously. I think they believe in safety; they believe in everybody going home to their family every day. My direct supervisors are very big on safety. They promote safety; they visit the crews*

*and make sure everybody's okay, make sure we're following
the rules.*

Jack also added that his leadership would stop work in progress to discuss potential hazards and risks: "If they see something that could be an imminent danger, they will stop us and talk to us about it." Jack concluded our interview by sharing that his experience with all his leadership was *more than following and enforcing safety rules*. He said, "They promote a safety culture that's not just safety and safety rules; that's driving, that's walking, talking, being on the phone, any procedure policy—all of that is addressed on a consistent basis in our yard."

Gerry described during his interview that he experienced his organizational leadership as supportive and his immediate management's safety culture and practices as "important, it's number one; the availability of anything that we need to be safe. They participate in our safety culture. I feel supported." He concluded the interview by elaborating on his immediate supervisor's safety involvement:

> *He's involved from the start of the day to the end of the day,
> and we thank him for it. He participates in all our safety
> meetings. He makes sure all of us get them—the safety
> bulletins; he's intimately involved. He makes sure we have
> all the tools and safety equipment that we need to be safe.
> I think the number one thing is he comes out and visits the
> crews and talks to us about being safe on a regular basis.
> And that's super, super important when it comes to our job
> because he's just involved in our job. He really is involved.*

In this section's introduction, I conceded that rule compliance is inherent and must be prioritized in the utility industry because the occupational hazards can be catastrophic and sometimes fatal. It was refreshing to hear the linemen share about a culture shift occurring in the organization that emphasized *all* aspects of safety, not only "rules and tools." The linemen's experience and perception aligned with my literature research related to how leaders set the tone for organizational culture.

Culture is *dynamic,* and it reflects the leaders' beliefs, language, behaviors, and practices, and it is transferred to others in the organization.[3]

> By creating a culture where the health and safety of employees is an uncompromised value and following up with action (leading by example), injuries will be prevented, and both employees and the company will flourish.

Through my interviews with the linemen, I learned that this "dynamic" (as described above) organizational culture had a powerful influence on their engagement. From the linemen's lens, prioritization of emergent work, poor program design, corporate hypocrisy, and the focus-on-safety-rules culture served as barriers to program participation; however, these linemen participated despite the organizational hurdles.

The research is spot-on that the health and safety of company employees should be the business of every leader, as the physical and economic burden resulting from injuries has a direct correlation to the company's bottom line. Leaders must be ready to see safety not only as a department but as a way of life.[4] By creating a culture where the health and safety of employees is an *uncompromised* value and following up with action (leading by example), injuries will be prevented, and both employees and the

---

[3] Clarke & Estes, *Turning Research.*

[4] Brian Fielkow, 2022.

company will flourish. The bottom line is that "our actions must become moving pictures of our beliefs."[5]

Prioritizing Emergent Work Over Safety

It was a typical day in the life of a utility lineman. The work for the day had been assigned, the linemen's pre-job briefing ("tailboard") was completed and understood, and the trucks were loaded and ready to go. What made this day slightly different, however, was that the drive to the work location and the weather was going to be extra challenging. There had been several fires throughout the state during this time, which made road accessibility difficult. The weather had been erratic, and there was a possibility of encountering snow-covered roads.

The combination of terrain and weather was reeking with potential safety hazards for the crews and the equipment. During my interview with lineman Thomas, he shared very candidly that, on this day, he was directed to head down one of the fire roads nearby despite the weather. Thomas said:

> *They actually wanted me to travel through some fire roads and forestry department roads that, if I got snowed in, I would get my truck stuck. And I would be out there in the middle of nowhere, with no radio or cell phone communication because it's out of range.*

Thomas also shared with me that he *knew exactly* what he had signed up for when he accepted this job. He knew that danger is "the nature of the beast" in this line of work; it's an occupational hazard, so to speak. This day was a little different, he said. The external forces of nature, such

---

[5] Bill Martin, 2023.

as weather and terrain, were a stark reminder that he would need to take extra heed to everything he had learned about safety. He also shared that he immediately thought about the daily safety protocol created to protect himself and the crew from injury. His experience in his career thus far was that the expectation was there that, even though the work was dangerous, the job must get done, and safety, unfortunately, was put on the back burner. He also shared with me that his mind couldn't help but wonder about the constant contradiction he'd experienced on several occasions, and this day was no different. In his experience and perspective, his supervisors, though they spoke of the importance of safety, pushed the idea that emergent work was always understood or perceived to override safety.

When I interviewed another lineman, William, his experience was almost identical to what Thomas had shared with me. William shared that if emergent work came up at seven in the morning, which is the time allotted to employees to perform the program exercises, work would come first. William said, "The injury-prevention (IP) program will be skipped over; our supervisors would say, 'You are getting right to your work.' And that happens all the time. Safety is not the number one priority, first thing in the morning."

Like Thomas, William described the mixed messages from the organizational leaders and his immediate supervisor by noting, "Now, the executives might say, we want safety, safety, safety, but the lower management is about production, production, production." William shared another factor about his experience in this hierarchical culture: If one of the linemen challenged his supervisor about not being allowed to perform the exercises because of work, the supervisor would say, "Hey, you can do the stretches later. Productivity and not canceling planned outages and a whole lot of other things take priority over safety." William and Thomas were not the only linemen who experienced these scenarios.

Another lineman I interviewed, Jack, shared with me that in the middle of performing the morning exercises, they were asked to stop because of work: "I'll be honest; sometimes we get rushed out to work and don't get to finish the exercises." Michael is another lineman I interviewed who shared the same experiences. He said:

> *If it's a really pressing job and high profile, we're willing to bend some of the safety rules or flat-out ignore them. Yeah, as long as no one gets hurt. And if one does (get hurt), then we are going to get in trouble for not telling them no. But they'll pressure you into breaking the rules (or bending them) to get stuff that they need done.*

Though their leadership generally espoused that health and safety was an organizational value and priority, in *their* experience, more value was given to production, performance, and emergent work. As my interviews progressed, I understood and empathized with their experience wholeheartedly. As one of the safety advisors who supported this organization, I, too, witnessed the focus on emergent work (on more occasions than I care to admit) and how it superseded their participation in the IP program. For example, I'd show up in the crew assembly room in the mornings, where they typically performed the exercises, only to find a couple of the guys participating and others gathered around chatting while the supervisors' focus was preparation for the day's work. Often, in the middle of the exercises, the guys had to scurry off to complete emergent work that was handed to them. The expectation, as I perceived and experienced it, was that the line guys had to drop what they were doing and get to work.

The literature I researched parallels with the interview responses that prioritizing performance and production does not support a proactive safety culture, nor does it support the value of program participation and the benefits it provides. When employees perceive that safety and health are not a priority to leadership because leaders' words and actions are incongruent, they experience corporate hypocrisy.[6] Corporate hypocrisy is characterized as the belief that when company leaders claim something yet do not demonstrate it in action, it becomes a barrier to employee engagement because it fosters resentment, distrust, and apathy for safety.

> When leaders minimize the importance of injury prevention because they choose to compromise safety and prioritize emergent work, both the employee and the company lose in the long run.

When leaders minimize the importance of injury prevention because they choose to compromise safety and prioritize emergent work, both the employee and the company lose in the long run. Employee lives suffer because of sprain and strain injuries for the company, while injury claims and health insurance premiums skyrocket. This takes me back to another Brian Fielkow quote about production or customer demands competing with safety. He shared in the NSC publication, "You can never allow these pressures to compromise safety."[7] Additionally, I believe that Mr. Fielkow's statements that I mentioned in this chapter's first section deserve another worthy and honorable mention:

If safety is truly a value, then we shouldn't compromise it.
We, as leaders, can influence what employees believe.

---

[6] Tillman Wagner, et al, "Corporate Hypocrisy: Overcoming the Threat of Inconsistent Corporate Social Responsibility Perceptions," *Journal of Marketing* 73, no. 6 (November 2009): 77–91, https://doi.org/10.1509/jmkg.73.6.77.

[7] Brian L. Fielkow, "The 2022 CEOs Who 'Get It,'" *Safety+Health Magazine*, January 23, 2022, https://www.safetyandhealthmagazine.com/articles/22097-ceos-who-get-it-2022.

The only thing I can add to this is we safety leaders must ingrain these statements in the forefront of our brains. Better yet, we must wear them on our heads just as we wear our PPE.

Because the linemen's safety matters and is a value to them, I was honored that all of the linemen spoke with me with such transparency. By their tone and demeanor, it was apparent to me that they were filled with gratitude and pride for their work. This clearly demonstrated that they did not take their positions lightly, and they considered it a privilege to be linemen. They all respected the hierarchy and did as they were instructed. Though I have always respected the difficult and dangerous nature of their jobs, after our interviews were over, I gained even more respect for their passion and dedication to their craft. Listening to these linemen's experiences and perspectives, I must consider that "respecting the hierarchy" of command and control modeled by leadership is part of the problem. This mindset contributes to a culture that perpetuates employees' fear of speaking up and challenging the status quo. If we are to change to really embrace safety, we have to encourage *everyone* to have a voice.

Leaderships' Lack of Participation in Injury Prevention Programs

Any lineman will tell you that their job is an *extremely* physical one that requires performing their work in compromising positions for extended periods, repetitively. They are *too* familiar with the aches and pains that accompany any typical day after a hard day's work. As a matter of fact, there is a moniker used throughout the linemen culture, "linemen-ectomy" (which comes with the job), and it refers to a lineman who suffers back pain while working or has possibly suffered a back injury. I first heard about this term over twenty years ago while giving a presentation about preventing back injuries. I remember this day as if it were yesterday. Some of the linemen stopped me dead in my tracks during my presentation and said, "Take it easy, Pollyanna. Don't you know that we suffer from linemen-ectomies? We always have and will have pain from our work. It's an occupational hazard." I was speechless that pain had been normalized in this culture. In retrospect, this encounter may have been the beginning of my deep desire to reverse the normalization of the pain culture in this organization.

One of my doctoral interview questions was designed to explore linemen's perception of the safety culture fostered by their *direct* supervisor. I asked the linemen what their direct supervisor communicated to them about the purpose of the IP program. Most of the linemen shared with me that their leaders did a great job verbally at communicating that the purpose of the program was to prevent injuries; however, what they demonstrated differed from what they said. Some linemen recalled their leadership describing the IP program as a safety program designed to prevent sprains and strains, while others described it as a program to help employees conduct difficult and repetitious work while in awkward body postures. The linemen's description of what their supervisors communicated to them about the IP program confirmed to me that their supervisors understood the purpose of the IP program.

When I interviewed lineman Chris, he said that his understanding of the program, as communicated by his leaders, was to "stretch prior to starting work, to loosen up the limbs a little bit, and stretch." Lineman Gerry shared that his immediate supervisor communicated the usefulness of the program more in-depth: "He probably did talk a lot about strains and sprains, and that it'll help prevent injuries." Michael shared with me that his immediate supervisor described the usefulness of the program: "It's to help keep your body injury-free." Lineman Henry shared that his immediate supervisor compared this program to a former program and rated it as a better one. His manager described this program as follows:

It's a better stretch program than what was previously used,
that it was a way, obviously, to monitor our movement
moving forward, good or bad, to monitor it and to focus
in on areas of concern or issues, be it a certain muscle, or
the back, the arm, the shoulder, the leg, the knee, to focus
on that. As it continued, it was a most definite dynamic
program that would change with time and with work, and
certain areas that may be sore or maybe it worked harder
than others, but it was basically a continuing dynamic pro-
gram that was going to help us better our stretching and
minimize injuries at work.

During my interview with Jack, he mentioned that the executive leadership communicated the purpose of the program: "It's for us, for our safety, to keep our bodies moving and to make sure we have a long and illustrious career without injury, without permanent damage to our bodies later on in life." Like Jack, lineman Thomas shared that his leadership communicated the program was for injury prevention, and leadership included specific job tasks:

Improving our mobility; our injury prevention should get
better because of the odd movements while we're on the
pole, off our hooks, or the amount of bending we're doing
from a bucket truck trying to reach certain work areas.

Unfortunately, most of the linemen shared a different story. They confided that their managers verbalized the purpose of the program; however, they demonstrated a lack of support for the program. Also, some shared their managers communicated to them that they doubted the program's benefits and that "it was a wasteful use of time." This was very concerning to me and reminded me of my experience with some of the managers over the years. All managers in the organizations I supported knew I was a huge advocate for this program. Sadly, on many occasions, I was stopped and confronted by them with comments such as, "You know, we have REAL work to do," "I work out at the gym before coming to work, so I don't need this," or "This is a complete waste of time."

Michael shared with me that his immediate supervisor communicated the program was for injury prevention; however, he also described receiving mixed messages from his supervisor. He recounted that his supervisor said to him, "Everything's got a purpose; everything's money driven. If they keep us healthy and it helps their bottom line, they're going to do it." Another lineman, Larry, shared that his supervisor said of the program, "It's a waste of time." Lineman John recounted that the message he received from the leaders about the program's usefulness was that "it's going to relieve some of the stress on the muscles and all the other body parts." He shared with me, however, "You know, Maria, my leaders' comments led me to believe they were not on board with the program."

> Employees will experience a reduced interest in program participation when there are low expectations of program benefits and a lack of leadership support.

After hearing their perspectives and experiences, it was evident there was a lack of leadership participation in the program *despite* their communication about the program's purpose. According to these linemen, there had been little to zero supervisor participation since the program's inception. During the interview, Michael commented about his supervisor: "Since he's been my supervisor, I've never seen him do it." Then Larry quantified his supervisor's participation: "My supervisor? Yeah, zero. Big fat zero."

Additionally, Larry's perception of leadership promoting the program as injury prevention yet not participating was "hypocritical behavior." Larry expressed adamantly the importance of leading by example and modeling desired behavior. I quoted Larry as saying, "It is very hypocritical for him to suggest we participate, then not participate himself. It's a problem because he is a leader, and I think it's a role that he should consider if he wants us to participate." Larry's words were powerful, confirming how essential it is for leaders to lead by example to obtain their employees' trust and validating my research about corporate hypocrisy.

Although I will cover COVID-19's impact on program participation in the next section, it is worthy of a mention here. Lineman John quantified his supervisor's participation in the program prior to COVID-19 was about 5 percent; however, he added:

> *A few times out of the week, I may have seen him participating, but then he would disappear or not participate with the group. He may have participated in the stretches with us occasionally in a meeting or when higher leaders were present. After COVID-19, I think it has been zero participation since, and it dwindled completely.*

During the interviews, all the linemen were very straightforward with me. They didn't hold back from sharing their perspectives. I was extremely mindful, appreciative, and impressed with their candidness to share their experiences as they related to the injury-prevention program. Their responses suggested to me that their supervisors failed to lead by example, and everything they shared with me aligned with the literature research I conducted related to factors that reduce employee interest in program participation. Employees will experience a reduced interest in program participation when there are low expectations of program benefits and a lack of leadership support.

From the linemen's perspective and experience, their leadership *did not* support the program because their words did not match their actions. They viewed it as hypocritical. More than one lineman shared, "If my supervisor says that the program will benefit me, then why don't *they* participate?"

As I also mentioned in a section above titled "Prioritizing Emergent Work Over Safety," employees experience corporate hypocrisy resulting from the inconsistency between their leaders' talk and walk, which "fosters resentment, distrust, and apathy for safety."[8]

If an organization's leadership espouses the value of an injury-prevention program, it is vital that the sentiment be followed up with action and echoed throughout the leadership ranks to encourage greater employee engagement and, in turn, greater return on investment.

> This disease does have a cure, and it's called leadership.

My perspective of corporate hypocrisy is that it's an insidious disease that destroys trust and relationships and consequently stifles the effort to foster and sustain a culture of trust and engagement. It doesn't have to be this way, however. This disease *does* have a cure, and it's called leadership. Leaders can eradicate corporate hypocrisy, but it comes with a price—consistency, commitment, intentionality, and values. Isn't employee safety and health worth it?

COVID-19 Impact and Program Design

In early 2020, the world as we knew it changed drastically. The COVID-19 pandemic affected lives drastically, disrupted work in ways never expected,

---

[8] Wagner, "Corporate Hypocrisy," 77–91.

and brought a new meaning to "working together." For the utility linemen in this organization, many standard operating procedures were altered, new work methods and program designs were created and implemented that adhered to COVID-19 restriction mandates, and, ultimately, the injury-prevention program was canceled in its entirety.

Changes in work design processes can create barriers to achieving organizational success. In my study's case, the changes in the usual program design protocols with the injury-prevention program resulting from the COVID-19 pandemic served as a barrier to employee participation. These barriers—such as access to a location that was available previously, time limitations placed on participation, and faulty synchronization between employee availability and program schedules—served as obstacles to employee participation in the program.

During my interviews, the linemen shared various challenges they experienced during the pandemic related to participation in the IP program. They were very candid with their thoughts and emotions about how COVID-19 restrictions impacted their lives, their work, and, ultimately, how the pandemic became a barrier to their participation in the IP program. They expressed disappointment for the inability to participate in the program collectively at the work district prior to heading out to conduct their daily work. Conversely, they shared how eager they were for the program to resume because of how positively the program impacted their physical well-being and, consequently, their work.

Linemen John, Henry, and William shared with me that COVID-19 restrictions caused operational challenges, such as a change in on-site reporting protocols, which consequently resulted in significant decreases in program participation. Since they no longer reported to their respective yard but instead had to report directly to the job site, collectively, they shared that as far as they were concerned, nobody was participating.

Two other linemen whom I interviewed, Larry and Thomas, shared that they were looking forward to the day when they could resume participation in the program. Larry expressed with emotion, "I'm a little saddened by it, and I'm eagerly waiting for the time when we can get back into the crew room where it's spacious and we can perform our stretches." Like Larry, Thomas shared that because of the restrictions, they were not able to perform their exercises in the office, and the outdoor terrain at their work location was not suitable, even though they had exercises that they could perform near their work trucks. He said:

> *We're not in a classroom setting anymore, especially due to COVID-19; we're on pods, and we're no longer at the office. We could do outdoor exercises at our trucks, but a lot of times, we're in an area where it's rocky or muddy.*

A couple of other linemen, Gerry and Michael, shared how the inability to participate in the program impacted their physical well-being. Gerry described it: "When this pandemic started, we stopped doing the stretching program. When we stopped doing it at work, I don't know about everybody else, but I really felt the difference." Similarly, Michael described his experience: "Well, when I was doing it, it helped me with some mobility issues I had, but ever since this COVID thing, they've stopped it."

Program design can serve as an obstacle to employee participation in an injury-prevention program. Potential barriers can be access to location, time limitations on participation, and faulty synchronization between employee availability and program schedules. And as the linemen shared with me, this became an issue during COVID.

After conducting the interviews, one of the common themes that emerged was directly related to research I found about the impact of poor program design. In this case, COVID did just that—it changed the entire landscape of how their work got done, including their morning exercise program, which ultimately affected employee engagement in the program.

As we know now, 2020, 2021, and part of 2022 were extremely unusual because of the pandemic. The company's resiliency was tested to levels never expected, which forced their standard operating procedures and program design to change drastically and repeatedly. To some extent, these utility linemen were considered the other "frontline workers"; after all, the power needed to stay on. It was crucial they adapted to every last-minute change in their workday, even when an abundance of program design barriers wreaked havoc on them in the midst of the pandemic.

Along with the entire world and this organization, I, too, was not prepared for the challenges that COVID-19 presented. I did not have COVID-19 literature relevant to my study, so there was no way to anticipate the impact it would have. It was a lesson learned that we will always have external forces outside of our control. To fully obtain and experience all of the benefits of a successful injury-prevention program, it is vital that organizations address these program design barriers and discover ways to mitigate or eliminate them so they don't impact the organization's safety culture they are trying to create.

Chapter Takeaways

- In order to create a culture where both employees and organizations flourish, leaders must connect with their employees by building and sustaining trusting relations with their employees.
- Create an organizational culture that sets the tone that will not compromise safety.
- Be a role model of the behavior desired (walk the talk) to engage your employees and transform your organizational culture.

Focus Questions

- What steps are you taking to connect with your employees to create trusting relationships?
- How well do you currently create a culture that does not compromise safety?
- In what ways do you communicate, reinforce, and model the value of your programs?

CHAPTER 2

KNOWLEDGE

Early last year, I attended a union representatives' conference in Southern California. The guest keynote speaker was leadership expert Jocko Willink, owner and founder of Extreme Ownership Academy. Jocko's leadership concepts and mission regarding employee safety ownership and accountability align with the direction the union is going, which is to inspire all union leaders to be accountable for their employees.

During his keynote, Jocko didn't pull any punches. He was dynamic, energetic, and impactful as he drove home the importance of leadership's role in an organization's safety culture. He reiterated that leaders MUST own safety and own it to the point of the extreme. What Jocko meant by this was that if there were any safety challenges or incidents/accidents in a company, the leadership, from frontline supervisors to the top of the "food chain," must take responsibility and own that they are responsible for *everything* that occurs under their watch.

He emphasized passionately that leadership MUST role model the behavior desired (walk the talk) if they want to change or engage their employees. It was an extremely powerful keynote speech, and as I looked around the wall-to-wall filled conference ballroom, heads were nodding in agreement with the knowledge that Jocko was passionately imparting. At one of the front-row tables, I was pleasantly surprised to see six executive leadership members from the utility company I referred to in my study. Immediately after the conference, the six met at their table for what appeared to be a debrief. Though the CEO of this utility company was not part of the six, he joined the union leadership for dinner later.

The union representatives who were present for this keynote were not the only ones nodding in agreement; mine was as well. I was ecstatic while listening to Jocko's keynote, and I felt like one of those bobblehead toys, with my head nodding uncontrollably. Everything he said with such passion and conviction aligned with my topic of study. He was speaking my language!

One of my biggest knowledge takeaways was how adamant Jocko was about leaders needing to take *extreme* ownership and responsibility and that they are responsible for *everything* that occurs under their watch. It was energizing to watch the union representatives, the union leadership, and the company leadership agree with Jocko.

While exploring research literature, I learned that *every seven seconds,* an employee is injured while working because of a sprain and strain injury. These injuries are the leading cause of nonfatal occupational injuries in private industry and local and state government. My research also revealed that there was an upward trend with sprain and strain injuries. In 2005, the leading injury across all United States industry sectors were sprains and strains, and they accounted for 41 percent of workplace injuries requiring days away from work.[9] In 2014, 80 percent of injuries

---

[9] US Bureau of Labor Statistics, "Sprains and Strains Again Among Most Common Workplace Injury," *The Economics Daily,* November 20, 2006, https://www.bls.gov/opub/ted/2006/nov/wk3/art01.htm?view_full.

to private industry workers were sprains and strains, and they accounted for 25 percent of workers' compensation costs, making for an economic burden of $15.1 billion annually.[10]

Another area of my research pertained to increasing and sustaining employee motivation and engagement. All arrows pointed to leadership—specifically, as it pertained to influencing and motivating employee participation in worksite programs. When leadership verbalizes and models enthusiastic support and participation for a company program, employees will engage.

Encountered Assumptions

When I embarked on this journey and decided to focus my dissertation topic on influencing and motivating employee engagement in company injury-prevention programs, I started with a variety of assumptions relating to why employees did or did not engage because of my experience as a safety professional in that organization. My first postulation pertained to why employees were not engaging in the injury-prevention program. During my twenty-year employment with the company, and more specifically, the last ten years as a safety professional supporting the linemen workforce, my perception was that employees did not participate because they lacked the knowledge that the program was designed to prevent and mitigate sprains and strains. Instead, I assumed they thought of it as an exercise or stretch program.

Secondly, I assumed leaders didn't support the program wholeheartedly because they minimized the value of it when they referred to it solely

---

[10] "Liberty Mutual Research Institute for Safety Releases 2014 Workplace Safety Index," *Business Wire*, January 14, 2015, https://www.businesswire.com/news/home/20150114005546/en/Liberty-Mutual-Research-Institute-for-Safety-Releases-2014-Workplace-Safety-Index.

as a "stretch program." Thus, I believed this caused the linemen to minimize the program's value as well. My assumptions resulted from my personal experience with the way the company introduced this program and its subsequent launch. Although the vendor had been very clear about the program's purpose as a *safety program* aimed at reducing, preventing, and mitigating sprains and strains, the leadership continued to refer to it as a "stretch program," and the workforce did the same.

On numerous occasions during pre-program launch meetings, I continued my "campaign" for a paradigm shift. I expressed that it was critical for this program's success that it was branded as a "safety injury-prevention program" instead of a "stretch program." I understand this may come across as a semantics issue, and you may ask yourself, "Why was it important *not* to refer to this program as a stretch program?" In my opinion, branding this program as a stretch program and not as a safety program minimized the program's value, consequently decreasing impact and hindering success.

> For program engagement, sustainability, and success, knowledge plays a critical role.

This stretch program frame of reference was entrenched in the organization's safety culture. For over twenty years, various programs were launched in the organization with the expectation that they would aid in the reduction of sprains and strains, yet they were always referred to as stretch programs. Several programs came and went, yet sprains and strains remained rampant in the company.

During my topic research, I discovered that for program engagement, sustainability, and success, knowledge plays a critical role. Equally critical, the program's purpose and vision must be communicated strategically and then disseminated across the company. To my surprise, after interviewing the linemen and hearing their perspectives and experiences, it became evident to me that the "knowledge mindset gap" was a factor for the leadership, not the linemen. The linemen were fully vested in the program despite their leadership's engagement or lack thereof. After completing the interviews and my dissertation, I realized there was a missed opportunity in terms of exploring knowledge gaps in addition to motivation and organizational gaps; hindsight is twenty-twenty.

Factual and Conceptual Knowledge

To explore and identify gaps that influenced employee participation in the injury-prevention program, I utilized the Clarke and Estes gap analysis conceptual framework.[11] This framework is a systematic and analytical method that helps to clarify organizational goals and identify the knowledge, motivation, and organizational gaps that impact behavior to attain such goals. Awareness and the identification of one's knowledge and skills gaps are necessary steps in the process of facilitating improvement and achievement of organizational performance goals. For this study, I used a *modified* Clarke and Estes gap analysis model that focused solely on the motivation and organizational factors. To exclude the knowledge gaps was a mutual decision between my dissertation chair and myself. As mentioned in the previous section, hindsight is twenty-twenty.

Factual and conceptual knowledge—such as what, when, why, where, and how employees can achieve goals—is foundational. According to Clarke and Estes, there are two conditions in which knowledge and skill enhancement are required for job performance and organizational success. First, when employees do not know how to achieve the organizational or performance goal (factual knowledge) that is expected of them, and second,

---

[11] Richard E. Clarke & Estes, Fred, *Turning Research into Results: A Guide to Selecting the Right Performance Solutions* (Charlotte, NC: Information Age, 2008).

when future challenges are anticipated and require new problem-solving methods or concepts (conceptual knowledge).

The first condition usually indicates that employees may need *additional* information or training to ensure knowledge transfer occurs. As I conducted my interviews with the linemen, I discovered that they, indeed, had acquired the knowledge needed to perform the exercise movements correctly. The injury-prevention program vendor had done an excellent job in providing them with the necessary education and training for their success in this program, which consequently debunked my first assumption that employees were not engaging because they lacked knowledge that the program was designed to prevent and mitigate sprains and strains.

The second condition indicates the need for *ongoing* training or perhaps advanced training. For this program's success, ongoing and advanced training needed to continue, and unfortunately, it did not, and it was not only due to the pandemic. Prior to my retirement, which was one year before the pandemic hit full force, I was informed the program would most likely not have a future because it had already begun to fall by the wayside.

Throughout my career as a safety professional, I witnessed leaders face challenges in implementing organizational change, specifically obtaining a reduction in sprains and strains. I learned that the pathway for obtaining specific organizational goals (e.g., reducing sprains and strains via the program) is the correlation between the alignment of achieving such goals with organizational structures and critical business processes (e.g., a steadfast commitment to this injury-prevention program).

It is critical for leaders to ask themselves questions such as, "What do we want to accomplish? What will success look like, and how will we accomplish it?"

As mentioned above, identifying and assessing knowledge and skill set gaps are foundational for organizational success; conversely, knowledge barriers hinder that process. In this organization, leadership involvement and support should have included branding the program by its purpose, as well as acknowledging that non-engagement in the program posed a safety risk to the field operations workforce. It is critical for leaders to ask themselves questions such as, "What do we want to accomplish? What will success look like, and how will we accomplish it?"

> It is critical for leaders to ask themselves questions such as, "What do we want to accomplish? What will success look like, and how will we accomplish it?"

When I asked my interviewees to describe what their organizational leaders and direct supervisors communicated about the purpose of the program, almost 70 percent responded that "the purpose of the program was stretching to prevent injuries." Though the leaders and direct supervisors communicated the usefulness of the program for injury prevention, the linemen shared they (the leaders) expressed doubt about the program's purpose and value. I'm still of the mindset that the use of correct terminology for the program would have changed leadership's perspective from seeing the program as "just stretching" to injury prevention.

It was clear to me, because of the linemen's responses in the interviews, that they indeed had conceptual knowledge about the program as an injury-prevention strategy. The linemen conceptualized that this program would provide solutions to their sprain and strain challenges, even though leaders were not consistent in effective communication, involvement, and support about the relevance of the program as an "injury-prevention strategy." Despite their leadership's knowledge barrier, the linemen were very self-motivated to participate because of the benefits they experienced, such as less pain while performing strenuous job tasks, improved mobility, and an overall improvement in their quality of life.

Dr. Maria Silva-Palacios

Policies and Procedures Gap—Employees Unaware of Participation Expectations Policy

The literature research I conducted pertaining to employee engagement stated that organizational change that produces a desired outcome happens when leaders focus, align, and integrate organizational practices, policies, and climate. To explore and discover whether existing policies influenced their participation, during the interviews, I asked the linemen if any policies existed that required or encouraged participation in the injury-prevention program. Six out of the nine interviewees reported that they were unaware whether such a policy existed. Five of the six linemen described that their leadership espoused such a policy; however, there was no enforcement of the espoused expectations. Their responses were almost difficult to believe; however, my experiences were identical to the linemen's responses. The reality is that loose and up-to-interpretation participation mandates existed, and each district "enforced" them independently.

One lineman I interviewed, John, shared that he did not recall if a policy existed even though they were paid and allotted thirty minutes to participate every morning prior to beginning their work shift. He said, "I don't remember any policy, but I know that everybody is given half an hour for the exercise in the morning." Additionally, John shared with me that the allotted time was loosely monitored. He said, "Whether you do the stretching or whatever it might be, you are allowed half an hour, and nobody's ever taken that away." John concluded by stating, "Besides any other encouragement or checking if you're doing it right or wrong, I haven't seen that from our supervision."

Michael, a lineman from another district, said he described the organization's leadership and his immediate supervisor as not holding employees accountable for participating, even though participation was supposedly mandatory. He said, "They don't hold you to that." He further shared that if employees did not participate in the program, they were told to prepare for the workday. He described his supervisors as telling him, "Be productive and go get your trucks. Start loading and getting them ready for the day's work." Michael also shared that the loose expectations for participation facilitated non-participation. He added, "You get out of stretching anyway." He concluded that, in his experience, the immediate supervisor *occasionally* observed their participation:

> *He just comes out of his office every so often to check if we're doing them. If his supervisor found the employees were not participating, he would tell us, "What are you guys doing? Shouldn't you be stretching?" So basically, he just comes and checks. But that's about as far as it goes.*

Thomas, a lineman from a district different from Michael's, said, "I don't know if it's an actual policy that we do this program, but they have definitely encouraged us to do it." He added that his immediate supervisor said, "The company is allowing you to do this program for the first half hour of the day, so why wouldn't you do it?" Thomas described his immediate supervisor as seeing value in the program; thus, participation was encouraged. He also noted that his immediate supervisor reiterated the benefit of the program as "something that's going to make you more mobile, make you less susceptible to injuries, and the company's paying you this time to go ahead and do it. Why wouldn't you want to?"

Additionally, Thomas shared with me that his immediate supervisor ensured participation with periodic observation and called it to their attention if the employees were not participating. He recounted his supervisor as saying, "Either you're in here, and if you're not stretching, then you need to be outside getting trucks ready, gathering tools and equipment." Thomas also shared with me that his supervisor reminded the employees they were on company hours if they did not participate.

He quoted his supervisor, "If you want that half hour of pay, then you need to be working. Otherwise, you should not be sitting down and on your phone. You need to be doing the program then." Thomas concluded our interview by sharing that he did not perceive the supervisor's verbal mandate as a policy—it was only a suggestion. He said, "That tells me that it's not mandatory. I don't think it is a policy if they're telling me we have a choice to either stretch or get ready for the workday."

Henry's experience was like Thomas's. Although Henry said he was not aware that a written policy existed, he described his immediate supervisor observing participation by walking around to each individual station and saying, "Hey you, what are you doing? Get up and stretch." Like herding the sheep. Larry is a lineman in Henry's district, and he reported that the extent to which his immediate supervisor encouraged participation was to remind employees by saying, "Okay, let's go out in the stretch room, take your thirty minutes, and get out there."

William from another district shared that he was well aware of the union's support of the program; however, he did not recall that there was a mandate. He said, "I don't think there's any policy. I know the union came out for a while and said they backed this program and that we should stretch and do this; this is what we're paid to do."

Additionally, they shared that the verbal mandate was interpreted by them as a *suggestion* for participation because they were given the option to either participate or prepare the work trucks for the daily work. These options given to them were perceived by them as a lack of personal responsibility and accountability for participation.

I was not surprised by the responses I gathered for this question. As part of my responsibility to each organization I supported in field operations, I had to visit locations to ensure employees were participating in the program and to offer support in case the linemen had specific questions about the exercises. What I found was a handful of linemen participating while others stood around talking, not engaging, smoking outside, or getting their trucks ready for the day's work.

After collecting and analyzing the responses to this question, my findings revealed that besides the company providing a thirty-minute pay incentive for the linemen to participate in the program prior to beginning their work shift and the occasional supervisor observations to ensure employees were performing the exercises, the consensus was they were unaware or could not recall if any written policies and procedures existed related to program participation expectations—a consistent policy, that is. Also, the linemen shared that, at best, it was a verbal mandate that was very loosely enforced.

The results of my interviews, my personal experiences as a safety professional supporting this workforce, and the interviews I conducted perfectly aligned with the research that I found about what it takes for successful organizational change to occur, or in this case, to meet the goal of reducing sprains and strains. Throughout my employment in this company, I served as a leader, co-leader, or collaborator with multiple teams aimed at addressing these injuries (e.g., common cause evaluation team, field ergonomics program review team, injury-prevention program overview team, and a sprain and strain mitigation team, just to name a few). The goal was to identify potential gaps in these programs and create an effective approach for providing solution recommendations to reduce the injury rate by 25 percent in two years. During this time, the sprains and strains in this organization had reached their peak and accounted for approximately 90 percent of the company's injuries. Additionally, 50 percent of the utility field employees reported in a survey that they were experiencing pain. Pain was a huge concern because their pain was an indicator of a "brewing" sprains/strain injury.

As I continued to work on these teams, we became increasingly frustrated. We believed that our findings and suggestions to reduce these injuries were not top safety priorities. We also were disillusioned that a formalized, uniform, and consistent approach to preventing them did not exist (e.g., multiple organizations were participating in various programs without any participation expectation mandate). The team felt that there was a lack of leadership engagement and support for the sprain and strain program (via role modeling) and no measures in place to drive accountability or effectiveness.

As I reflect on my study findings and the findings from all the teams I was involved in during my employment, it validates my research that employee engagement and organizational change that produces a desired outcome happens when leaders focus, align, and integrate organizational practices, policies, and climate, and then align them to the company or organizational goals.

At the risk of sounding like a broken record, organizational change that produces a desired outcome happens when leaders focus, align, and integrate organizational practices, policies, and climate and then align them to the company or organizational goals. With respect to this organization's safety goals, leaders must focus on the alignment and integration of organizational practices and policies with organizational goals. Doing so will foster the cultural climate for employees to buy in, engage in programs, and, ultimately, for an organization's success in preventing and reducing these injuries. In other words, "If you plant corn, you get corn."[12]

Leadership Knowledge Gaps – The Real Issue?

I shared in the above section that while conducting the literature research portion for my dissertation, I came across data illustrating the upward trend of sprain and strain injuries. As you read, the results were alarming. What it also confirmed is that this organization in my study was not alone

---

[12] Martin, 2023.

in the struggle. The data showed that across the country, throughout various industry sectors, workers suffer sprain and strain injuries *every seven seconds*. In local and state governments and in the private industry, sprains and strains were the leading cause of nonfatal occupational injuries. As I continued my literature research, I learned that sprains and strains cause an economic burden on companies and a physical burden on the employees who work there.

For example, in 2013, one of five injuries treated in a medical facility was a sprain or strain, and these were the most common and costly injuries that affected all age groups.[13] In 2014, these injuries resulted in 25 percent of workers' compensation costs and a $15.1 billion annual economic burden.[14] Research I found also indicated that in 2018, 124 million Americans over the age of eighteen suffered sprain and strain injuries that were treated in healthcare facilities. In my quest to explore what companies were doing to mitigate this, I found that employers across the nation had implemented various worksite programs to address the economic burden and reduce worker injuries caused by sprains and strains.

I discovered, unfortunately, that 50 to 75 percent of employees do not participate in these worksite programs.[15] As I mentioned in the section above, in the organization I studied, real knowledge barriers existed within the leadership and not the linemen. It was impressive that the linemen were very self-motivated to participate because of the value and benefits they experienced despite leadership's knowledge barriers.

Leadership is the key. They set the tone for the entire organization. My

---

[13] Jaimo Ahn, MD, et al, "Sprains and Strains," *The Burden of Musculoskeletal Diseases in the United States*, https://www.boneandjointburden.org/fourth-edition/vb22/sprains-and-strains.

[14] "Liberty Mutual," *Business Wire*, 2015.

[15] Gena M. Fletcher, "Barriers and Enabling Factors for Work-Site Physical Activity Programs: A Qualitative Examination," Journal of Physical Activity and Health 5, no. 3 (May 2008), https://pubmed.ncbi.nlm.nih.gov/18579919/.

research related to the influence of leadership on employee participation in worksite programs confirmed my assertion. In this organization, I heard very frequently, "As the leader goes, so does the culture." These are profoundly true words because leaders are the bridge to the gap between successfully supporting and executing an injury-prevention program and the physical and economic burden caused by these injuries. Employees will embrace a program and will model their leaders' behavior if leadership is enthusiastically supportive. Additionally, to achieve 100 percent employee engagement, leaders must promote and engage the program and must be held accountable for their performance.

In the section below, I share the various ways sprains and strains impact a company economically and the employees' livelihood. The severity of sprains and strains vary and cause significant burdens for both company and employees, and they warrant research equivalent to the burden they pose to absenteeism, loss of productivity, workers' compensation costs, and employee health.

Absenteeism

The research revealed that in 2015, 37 American adults per 100 reported a sprain and strain injury, and these injuries resulted in days away from work.[16] Sprains and strains affect various body extremities. Studies revealed that, in 2015, back pain due to a sprain and strain injury caused approximately 264 million lost workdays in the United States, which was equivalent to two lost days of work per every full-time worker.[17] Absenteeism harms both the worker and the work. Lost time from work

---

[16] US Bureau of Labor Statistics, "News Release: Nonfatal Occupational Injuries and Illnesses Requiring Days Away from Work, 2015," November 10, 1016, https://www.bls.gov/news.release/osh2.nr0.htm.

[17] "Epidemiology of Musculoskeletal Disorders in the United States," *NIH National Library of Medicine*, accessed January 19, 2024, https://www.ncbi.nlm.nih.gov/books/NBK559512/.

leads to a loss of knowledgeable and experienced workers. Additionally, lost time from work leads to a need for schedule extensions, which impedes the ability to meet project deliverables by their deadlines.

Loss of Productivity

Loss of productivity was another burden as a result of sprains and strains, and it is a byproduct of absenteeism. Research revealed the increasing trend of loss production resulting from absenteeism. In 1995, a study about lower back sprains and strains showed that back pain was the major cause of productivity loss for United States workers.[18] Research in 2011 revealed that productivity costs resulting from absenteeism were greater than healthcare costs, and there was a $132 billion loss for workers who suffered a neck or back injury. In 2017, sprains and strains were the leading cause of work-related injuries, which resulted in a $104 million loss in productivity.

Workers' Compensation Costs

Another burden that companies experience because of these injuries is the high worker compensation costs. Workers' compensation claims filed in 2020 and 2021 indicated that sprain and strain injuries averaged $34,293 per worker annually.[19] In 2014, they placed an economic burden on workers' compensation of $15.1 billion and accounted for 25 percent of workers' compensation costs.[20] In 2018, they accounted for $13.7 billion in workers' compensation costs, which is 25 percent of the entire national burden.[21]

[18] How-Ran Guo, et al, "Back Pain among Workers in the United States: National Estimates and Workers at High Risk," *Am J Ind Med* 28 no. 5 (November 1995): 591–602, https://pubmed.ncbi.nlm.nih.gov/8561169/.

[19] "Workers' Compensation Costs," *NSC Injury Facts*, https://injuryfacts.nsc.org/work/costs/workers-compensation-costs/.

[20] "Liberty Mutual," *Business Wire*, 2015.

[21] "The 2018 Workplace Safety Index from Liberty Mutual," *WCInsights*, https://wcinsights.com/the-2018-workplace-safety-index-from-liberty-mutual/.

Employee Health

Adults report sprains and strains injuries more than any other medical condition. Consequently, when a person suffers a sprain and strain injury, their health and life are affected. Because of the pain caused by these injuries, routine activities such as getting dressed, meal preparation, bathing, and walking become limiting and difficult to accomplish. Sprains and strains also worsen preexisting medical conditions. For example, if a person suffers from diabetes or hypertension, a sprain or strain limits their ability to get the daily activity needed to manage the preexisting medical condition.

> Leadership support and participation are the key. Leaders must be participatory, supportive, and enthusiastic regarding the program.

Clearly, the financial stakes are high for companies that do not focus on the knowledge gaps that hinder employee engagement in injury-prevention programs. The statistics speak for themselves! Addressing these obstacles will lead to achieving the goal of 100 percent employee engagement. *Leadership support and participation are the key.* Leaders must be participatory, supportive, and enthusiastic regarding the program. They must have integrity and lead by example to foster employee trust that the company and organization do not care more for productivity than their health and safety. Finally, leaders must model the behavior they desire to foster and sustain, be passionate about the change effort, align their goals with those of the organization and company, and, as Jocko Willink stated so passionately, do it with "extreme ownership."

I've addressed the importance of overcoming obstacles that stifle employee engagement and prevent employees from remaining injury-free while keeping leadership from attaining desired organizational deliverables. In this next section, I will cover the motivational factors that increase employee engagement and share the linemen's personal testimonies that motivated them to continue performing the program exercises despite the obstacles they faced before and during the pandemic.

Chapter Takeaways

- Be aware that the financial stakes are high for leaders who are not aware of knowledge gaps that hinder employee engagement in injury-prevention programs.
- Your support and participation in injury-prevention programs are critical for success. As a leader, you must have a steadfast commitment and extreme ownership of your employees' health and safety.
- Organizational change, employee engagement, and the desired organizational outcomes will be achieved when you, as a leader, focus, align, and integrate organizational practices, policies, and climate.

Focus Questions

- Are there any knowledge gaps that could be hindering employee engagement in your injury-prevention programs?
- What steps are you taking to ensure there is a focus and alignment on an integrated approach of organizational practices, policies, and climate to reduce sprains and strains in your organization?
- Are you asking yourself and your organizational leaders, "What do we want to accomplish, what will success look like, and how will we accomplish it?" If so, how often?

CHAPTER 3

MOTIVATION

"I feel better, and it makes life better," Thomas shared, with a smile and an upright and confident posture during our interview.

I nodded and smiled, encouraging him to continue.

"Doing the injury-prevention program means less pain. A lot of times, I had back issues. So, after doing the program exercises, they strengthened my back and core, and that has resulted in better movement. I have better balance." He quickly added, "Especially as the workforce is getting older and the daily tasks that we do over and over, it's just better overall."

He shifted in his chair and continued, "Because of the program, I feel like I did when I first started as a lineman. I've gained all the movements I had before." He concluded by noting the benefits to his home life, saying he enjoyed playing with his kids. "I just feel overall better."

Thomas had a high level of perceived value in the injury prevention program, and it showed.

One of the constructs used in my doctoral study was motivation. The research question designed to explore this was, "What do employees perceive as potential factors that can motivate them to participate in the injury-prevention program in their work?" People engage in just about anything when they perceive that participating in an activity has value. Clarke and Estes affirmed that motivation is important because it is the driving force behind the desire to complete tasks; consequently, when employees perceive a program as valuable, they are motivated intrinsically and will engage in the task or behavior.[22]

> People engage in just about anything when they perceive that participating in an activity has value.

| Value

I explored the linemen's value perceptions about engaging in the organization's injury-prevention program. I mentioned in this chapter's introduction that what a person perceives as valuable will predict their decision regarding what to engage in, persist at, or invest their mental effort into. Everyone is unique and is motivated in various ways. Motivation propels business success because it uncovers what a person values, then connects them to the benefit of achieving business goals and increases their work commitment.[23] This point was proven solidly in the linemen's testimonials in the section above.

---

[22] Clarke & Estes, *Turning Research.*

[23] Clarke & Estes, *Turning Research.*

While I'm on the topic of motivation, and before I continue, allow me to share motivation's foundation. Another framework I used in my dissertation was the expectancy value theory of motivation. This framework assesses, interprets, and evaluates what propels employees to make decisions, their persistence, and mental effort to perform a task or behavior.[24]

Expectancy Value Theory of Motivation

Expectancy value theory served as an effective model for me to explore what specific extrinsic and intrinsic factors motivated the linemen to participate in the injury-prevention program. Perceived value was one of the factors in my study that influenced engagement, and as we know now, it is an intrinsic motivator that influences employee engagement. Employees will engage in a task or behavior if they believe it provides value to themselves and others. Motivation involves three indicators: *active choice*, *persistence*, and *mental effort*, and I will dive into these three below.

The first motivational indicator, active choice, is characterized by an intentional action to complete a work goal or behavior. The linemen in my study manifested their active choice with their intentionality. They acknowledged and experienced the value and then committed to participation. Persistence, the second motivational indicator, is the decision to continue pursuing a goal despite any distractions or challenges. The linemen's persistence was demonstrated clearly throughout my time with them in the field. They participated in the program despite their perceptions of the organization's leadership, challenges resulting from subsequent cancellation of the program due to organizational barriers, and the significant obstacles that COVID-19 introduced. Once a person chooses a

---

[24] Chun-Fang Chiang & SooCheong (Shawn) Jang, "An Expectancy Theory Model for Hotel Employee Motivation," *International Journal of Hospitality Management* 27, no. 2 (June 2008): 313–322.

goal and is tenaciously persistent to complete it, they decide how much of the third motivational indicator, mental effort, they will invest in order to complete the goal. The linemen were tenacious (an understatement) about the mental effort they invested as demonstrated by their excitement to share their acquired knowledge with their families.

I shared in the previous chapter that I embarked on this journey with assumptions relating to why employees did or did not engage in the injury-prevention program. Also, I had my own biases. In my opinion, this was one of *the best* programs I'd experienced, and I was confident of the value it would bring to this organization's workforce; however, because I had personally encountered engagement barriers during the initial launch, I assumed the linemen didn't value the program. Was I ever wrong!!!

During the interviews, the responses to my question designed to explore their perception of the program's value were impressive and made my heart smile. Almost 70 percent of the linemen shared that they perceived the program to be of *significant* value. They expressed with passion that their program participation contributed to decreased body pain, improvement in their physical well-being, and lowered their risk of injury. Additionally, they said the program provided value beyond work *and* benefited their home life.

> "Why wouldn't I want to do it? It's something that's going to make me more mobile and less susceptible to injury."

Active Choice

I saw evidence of active choice, the first motivational indicator, as I heard story after story of the linemen in my study expressing their intentionality with the injury-prevention program. It was clear they valued the program due to the many benefits they were experiencing, and they chose day after day to continue to participate.

Christopher, a lineman from one location, shared that it wasn't only a tool to stretch. He said he learned information in the program that he shared with family and friends, such as nutrition and lifestyle changes. He said, "I use it as a tool to educate myself and my family to diet, like eating properly, taking care of our bodies, and how the body works so we can exercise or even eat healthier."

Jack, a lineman in Christopher's location, added that the program could add years to their careers as utility linemen (which I learned was SO important to these guys. They REALLY took pride in their work and careers). Jack said, "You can gain longevity from the use of your body and body parts. This is a strenuous job. You use every ounce of your body tissue, muscle, and joints, and they hurt." Another lineman, Henry, added that the program helped with his body because of the awkward body positions while working:

> *We just work in funky positions. We put our bodies through hard paces. It's more a realization, too, at my age to say, hey, I gotta take care of my body a little better. The value in it was health, longevity, and physical care for my body right now.*

Thomas, who was featured in the opening story, shared additional perks of participating in the program. He said that the program helped him conduct his work in a safer manner: "I work in awkward positions daily. These exercises help reduce the risk of getting injured because of all the different ways that we're contorting our bodies every day, so there was no reason not to participate." He added, "Why wouldn't I want to do it? It's something that's going to make me more mobile and less susceptible to injury."

Gerry expressed the same sentiments as Thomas and added that he believed the program would add years to his life. THIS blew my mind and made me smile ear-to-ear!! He said, "By going through the program every day, my body feels so much better. I believe I'll live longer. I'll give you a statement: I'll live longer." He concluded the interview by adding, "My flexibility, my back doesn't hurt as much; I'm more energetic because of it."

In all cases, the linemen demonstrated active choice. They experienced physical and psychological benefits and articulated those benefits to me with passion. Their responses also eliminated the biases I had. Also, the program impacted them so positively that they chose (actively) to share with their families and friends. Their candid answers validated my research pertaining to value as an intrinsic motivator. Once a person uncovers what they value, they are motivated intrinsically, which results in an increased work commitment and, in this case, participation in the program.

> Once a person uncovers what they value, they are motivated intrinsically, which results in an increased work commitment and program participation.

Persistence

From their responses in the interviews, it was evident to me that the linemen exhibited incredible persistence, the second motivational indicator. Despite the way they perceived the organization's leadership support or challenges with cancellation of the program or barriers due to COVID, the linemen persisted with the injury-prevention program. Again, they valued the physical and psychological benefits they were experiencing because of the program, and this led to intrinsic motivation to continue regardless of external factors.

Lineman Larry, as I refer to him, shared that he experienced body issues in the past and that participation in the program alleviated them. He said:

> *I've had some hip issues that I think now I've gotten health-ier, as far as mobility-wise. I had some back issues, and it was just like a car wearing down. I was showing similar signs, and once I started doing a variety of these exercises, little by little, a lot of that stuff just went away.*

Larry raved that by participating in the program, "You'll strengthen your back; you'll strengthen your abs and core." He continued that because of his participation in the program, he avoided injuring other body parts, "like putting my arm out of the socket. I can associate the usefulness of it because of the things that we do at work." Larry ended the interview by noting, "By participating in the program, it's going to make you more valuable to the company and less apt to get hurt."

Mental Effort

Another benefit the linemen shared with me was the value that the vendor's quality checks (QCs) provided. This really surprised the heck out of me as well. Remember I stated in the intro above that I had biases? Here's another one. I was convinced that the vendor QCs were a nuisance to the guys because they interrupted their work. On *many* occasions when I visited a location because I knew the vendor would be conducting a QC, I encountered visible displays of disinterest, such as eyes rolling, tobacco chewing, and sitting in the back of the room with sunglasses on and arms crossed. Sometimes, their body language was accompanied by blatant verbal disapproval, with comments such as, "Another QC? We have work to do," or the *famous*, "I already worked out at the gym this morning, so I don't need this." I heard their messages loud and clear!

However, despite their physical and verbal expressions of disapproval, and to my surprise yet again, *over half* of the linemen interviewed expressed that they were willing to invest a great deal of mental effort, the third motivational indicator, to engage in the program. Difficult to believe after my shared experience above, right? One lineman, John, reported that "more of the program instructors visiting the work locations would have been more helpful with participating because he could talk about certain injuries, certain body aches and pains." John added:

> *The personal touch made it feel like this was for me, and because of that, I was going to dig my teeth into this thing. It became more important and relevant to me in terms of my acceptance and participation in it. It's like having a teacher and the student, and if you let the student just do it themselves, they lose track, they lose interest. If they would've showed up a little more often, I think I would have been a lot more engaged.*

William, from another location, shared his interest in increased quality checks because it "made it a lot easier to participate when they would show up once a week and correct you if you're doing something wrong or show you a better way to do it." Henry shared the same sentiments as William, expressing, "I wish they would do more of the program coaches or if the teachers could come out more and work with the guys." He concluded the interview by noting, "That's when I started to buy in more; it was with the personal touch, and it made it more personal about my issues."

Here it is, in *their* words. Not only did they believe the program had value, but that it had *so much value* that they wanted more vendor quality checks; they also believed the program was going to make them more valuable to the company—wow!! In this organization, leaders espoused health and safety as a value and priority; however, as it related to participation in the injury program, the linemen's responses revealed that, in their perception, more value was given to production and performance. Unfortunately, leadership's prioritization of performance and production did not reinforce the value of participation in the program and the physical and psychological benefits it provided.

The wonderful reality is that the linemen recognized the program's value because of the physical and psychological benefits, not only for them but for their families and friends. It was evident they held the program in high regard. They shared their views of the QCs as personal coaching sessions and an opportunity to discuss their specific pain and injuries, proper body alignment, and exercise technique. Also, the guys believed that the quality checks facilitated and sustained their belief in the program's value and confirmed that they served as motivating factors for their participation. They just wished they had the program and more QCs, of course.

In all cases, the linemen clearly demonstrated the three motivational indicators: active choice, persistence, and mental effort. They experienced physical and psychological benefits for themselves and for their families and friends and articulated this with enthusiasm that truly surprised and inspired me. My heart was full.

Chapter Takeaways

- Know how to motivate your employees; it is critical for achieving business success because it uncovers what your employees value. Motivating your organization will connect them to the benefit of achieving business goals and increase their work commitment and engagement.
- Be cognizant of your employees' perceived value of your company's injury-prevention program(s). Your employees will invest a great deal of active choice, persistence, and mental effort to engage despite any challenges they experience.
- As a leader, do not prioritize performance and production over your employees' safety and health.

Focus Questions

- How are you inspiring motivation in your organization to engage your employees in injury-prevention programs?
- What steps are you taking to remove engagement barriers, such as production prioritization, to achieve 100 percent engagement?
- How are you communicating and modeling the value of your injury-prevention programs?

CHAPTER 4

SELF-EFFICACY

Though I witnessed many linemen struggle in performing the assessments for the injury-prevention program, one guy stands out: Michael. From the beginning, he was outspoken about his disapproval of the program. In true form of this organization's mix of bravado and playful culture, Michael teased many of the guys during their initial assessments that the injury-prevention program vendor conducted as a baseline within each group at each location. He continuously said how he could do them with his eyes closed, rolled his eyes constantly, and bottom line—he said it was bull*#!t!

Yet, this was the *same* guy who tapped me on the shoulder the day of his initial assessment and asked if I could chat alone. We walked away from the assembly room, and he asked if he could possibly be assessed in private. Very quietly, he added, "I'm afraid that I won't be able to get up from the floor." I was speechless!! I thanked him for his vulnerability and said I was honored he trusted me enough to be so candid. I asked the vendor if we could accommodate this lineman's request. He was assessed in private.

In a previous chapter, I wrote about factors that influence employee participation in company programs, specifically how lack of awareness, knowledge, and skill are potential organizational barriers. In chapter three, I dove into the expectancy value theory of motivation. To recap, expectancy value theory is a framework that assesses, interprets, and evaluates what propels employees to make decisions, their persistence, and their mental effort to perform a task or behavior. Motivation is important because it is the driving force behind the desire to complete tasks. For an increase in participation to occur, employees need to believe they are capable of fully participating in an activity. In this study, the linemen needed to have self-efficacy about executing the exercises, which they did. Though I will elaborate on this concept later in this chapter, self-efficacy is the belief that one has the capacity to perform a specific activity or behavior for a specific outcome.

I want to touch on more assumptions I had when I embarked on this journey. Because of my experiences with some linemen while I was employed with the company, I assumed they lacked the capability of performing the exercise movements prescribed by the program vendor. Throughout the years, I encountered linemen who could not perform the exercise, so their resistance to the program was based on that.

This brings back memories and validates why I had these assumptions that they did not feel capable of performing the prescribed exercises. I can recall so vividly when the program was launched, and the vendor visited several locations to conduct the initial seven physical assessments. These assessments were designed as a screening tool to evaluate the linemen's movement patterns in various body parts and to determine whether there was any pain associated while performing the assessments. The pain assessment was a critical program component because pain usually is a precursor to potential injury. One of the unique benefits of this program was that each exercise prescription was created based on the individual assessment results, meaning the program met each lineman where their capabilities were at that moment. Thankfully for Michael (the lineman from the opening story), this wasn't a "one-size-fits-all" program; it met his unique needs.

A few takeaways from that experience with Michael. First, employees' motivation to participate is diminished if they do not believe they can execute something; my research confirms this assertion. I can now understand Michael's concern more clearly and acknowledge the implications of his inability to perform the assessments. In this linemen culture, pain and performing their job coexist—it's an occupational hazard.

Over the years, the linemen shared with me (more like reminded me, repeatedly) that pain is something that "came with the job" because of the task repetition, awkward postures held for extended periods, and long years of service. Remember that I shared above in another chapter how the linemen coined the term "linemen-ectomy"? And even if I laughed because they referred to me as "Pollyanna," I was saddened by their normalization of pain. I was confident they could live pain-free. And, as you've read in their own words, they were able to experience pain-free work. I call that SUCCESS, wouldn't you? By the way, Michael wasn't the only lineman to ask for private assessments—all requests were granted. Michael's fear of his inability to perform the exercises was masked by his disapproval of the program and teasing of the linemen who did participate. Another point to consider is that in the linemen's eyes, not being able to execute the assessments or the prescribed exercises and requiring modifications implied that they would be deemed incapable of meeting the required physical work demands; hence, Michael's fear disguised as disapproval.

Third, another area of my research about the underlying factors that drive individual motivation is the significance of collective beliefs, experiences, and perceptions regarding the potential of being effective. To tie in the first motivation construct, value, with this section, I will share my findings about another intrinsic motivational construct that I mentioned briefly above, self-efficacy.

To further explore motivation, I researched Albert Bandura's theory of self-efficacy. Bandura posited that at the core of human behavior is the desire to be effective.[25] The motivation and commitment to accomplish goals, the mental effort a person chooses to invest to achieve them, and the persistence to overcome challenges in the face of distraction are influenced by how positively or pessimistically the person thinks and believes. Research in the healthcare industry shows that self-efficacy increases self-care behaviors. This is not merely a self-confidence issue, which is commonly mistaken for self-efficacy. Self-confidence has more to do with one's positive self-esteem, whether one believes in themselves or not, or the ability to do something. Whereas self-efficacy is the ability or competency to execute a specific task.

During the interview, my participants were asked how they felt about their ability to perform the injury-prevention exercises correctly, and 100 percent of the linemen reported they mastered the program exercises and had high levels of self-efficacy. Now I understand why the quality checks were so valuable to them. They served as a conduit to mastering the exercises, which increased their self-efficacy and consequently served as ongoing motivation to participate.

I remember one lineman, Jack. He rated his ability to perform the exercises numerically. He said, "I feel, for the most part, I would give it a

---

[25] Albert Bandura, "Self-Efficacy: The Foundation Of Agency," In W. J. Perrig & A. Grob (Eds.), *Control of Human Behavior, Mental Processes, and Consciousness: Essays in Honor of the 60th Birthday of August Flammer* (New Jersey: Lawrence Erlbaum Associates Publishers, 2000), 17–33.

90 to 95 percent ratio that I can effectively perform all they've given us." Henry attributed his self-efficacy to the quality checks and education he received from the vendor. He reported that his ability to perform the exercises correctly was due to his attention to proper technique, desire to master the exercises, and practice. He noted, "In anything, the more you do it, the better you get. Form is everything, so I tried to pay attention to it. But I wanted to get better and wanted to do better."

Another lineman named Christopher reported he mastered the exercises including the more difficult exercises. He said, "I found no problem whatsoever in any of the exercises, sometimes even some of the exercises that were above my grade." Like Christopher, John shared:

> *I feel pretty good. I think I mastered some of the basic moves and timewise, I think half an hour, that's what they're giving to us at work. I'll start with my hands, then my back, the roller, then the other exercises. Depending on the phase, I kind of really master a few of those and stick to them.*

All the linemen's responses confirmed to me that they had high levels of self-efficacy, and clearly, they believed it served as a motivating factor for their participation in the program. The biggest takeaway and "aha" moment for me was when they confidently shared about their mastery of the exercises, they attributed this to their attention to proper technique, their desire to master the exercises, and practice, practice, practice.

One important thing I want to add is that the linemen who responded with the *most* enthusiasm and motivation about participation were those whose direct supervisors participated alongside them on a daily basis; do you see the connection? Leaders can nurture self-efficacy, reinforce collective efficacy, and encourage engagement by creating a positive team environment that encourages commitment to the well-being of the group.

Chapter Takeaways

- Self-efficacy increases self-care behaviors. Acknowledge, embrace, and own your power to influence and nurture self-efficacy and collective efficacy.
- Encourage engagement by creating a positive team environment that encourages commitment to the well-being of the group.
- Ensure you are not normalizing a "pain culture," which predisposes your employees for injury.

Focus Questions

- In what ways are you communicating and reinforcing your commitment to the collective well-being of your team?
- How are you utilizing your influence to create a team environment that fosters and nurtures self and collective efficacy?
- What steps are being taken to deconstruct cultural norms that hinder success in your organization?

CHAPTER 5

AUTHENTIC LEADERSHIP

Bob made my work SO challenging. He was a nice man and very well respected in the organization because of his years in this line of work and his valuable knowledge. However, Bob didn't trust the leadership or the company, and he was very vocal about it. In each safety meeting that I facilitated, and for every idea I had about improving their safety, he always had a comeback about how it would never work . . . *every* idea.

When I expressed concern about him to the leadership team, they brushed me off and said, "Don't worry about him; you'll never win him over." Of course, if anyone knows me, they will attest that the word "never" rarely exists in my vocabulary. I decided that I was going to make every attempt to get to know him. I developed a genuine curiosity about him and wanted to gain an understanding of why he felt the way he did. I knew it wouldn't be easy, and it wasn't at first.

I sought him out every opportunity I had—on a crew visit, after a meeting, pretty much every time I could. I asked for his opinion about specific work processes and protocols. This was perfect because, as a new safety professional, I had little knowledge of what they did. I quickly noticed that he truly enjoyed my inquiries because, like most linemen, they take immense pride in their work and love to share about what they do. It wasn't long before I asked him to share his thoughts about the much-needed work processes at the next safety meeting. He responded emphatically, "Hell no, I hate speaking in public, and I'm not going to stand up in front of everyone." I reassured him he wouldn't have to and that he could speak from his seat (which was usually the last seat in the back row).

At the next meeting, we did just that. I'll never forget. I had everyone turn their chairs around toward the back of the room, and Bob spoke from his seat. It was one of the *best* meetings. In fact, it was much like the old commercial "when EF Hutton talks, everyone listens" moment. Everyone listened to what Bob had to say. He had a deep voice that matched his personality, yet there was something reassuring and calming about the way he presented his material. The meeting was a success, and I think Bob really enjoyed it too (although I'm sure he'd deny it). Also, I think people were a little shocked when he spoke at the meeting. After the meeting, a few of the employees, including leaders, asked me how I had convinced him to speak up in a safety meeting. My response was simple in theory, "I took an interest in him and his perspective." We continued this strategy of having Bob speak from the back of the room for a few more meetings. That's about the time I noticed a shift in Bob's personality. He was more engaged and volunteered to share his wisdom more and more. He had great ideas, and everyone welcomed his input.

Months later, someone shared with me that Bob was taking care of his wife, who was terminally ill. My heart ached for him. Gaining this information about him gave me more insight and empathy about who he was and, more so, why he presented himself the way he did. Soon after I found out about his wife, she passed away. I attended the funeral and approached him to give him my condolences. I could tell he was taken aback by my presence because of the way he looked at me when he saw me. He thanked me profusely for attending.

✦✦✦✦✦

Time had passed after the funeral, and it was time for another safety meeting. After this meeting, I was feeling a bit defeated because I was dealing with a lot of resistance from the leadership about safety protocols that needed to change and/or be implemented, and they weren't buying in. I was about to leave for the day and heading to the parking lot. Bob was in the parking lot near my car—leaning against the wall with his dark sunglasses on and smoking a cigarette. He stopped me and said:

> *Hey, you—I just want to let you know, for whatever it's worth, that you have all the crews' respect. We know that you have integrity, you care about us, and you just want to keep us safe. Thank you for this and for what you do.*

WOW and WOW, small victories make it all worth it! I'll never forget *this* moment. This time, I thanked *him* profusely. I shared with him that he had made my day because it had been a tough one. I got in my car and sat there contemplating his words. Then I realized that regardless of how defeated I felt in my job at times, Bob's words were a reminder of *why* I did what I did. It was about the people in the organization who I wanted to keep safe. I truly cared for each of them, and I made every effort to get to know them. Consequently, I gained their trust, and they worked *with* me toward the common goal of keeping everyone safe. It was truly a team effort.

Perhaps you're familiar with the famous quote often attributed to Peter Drucker: "Culture eats strategy for breakfast." In essence, Mr. Drucker is suggesting that it does not matter how "effective" a strategy is; the company's (or organization's) success depends on the culture. I would add to Mr. Drucker's quote: Culture eats strategy for breakfast . . . and the leaders create *that* culture. If you're a leadership enthusiast, as you've been reading to this point, you've probably connected the dots about the correlation between employee engagement and leadership. It is what I was alluding to in the previous chapter when I wrote about the linemen who responded with the most enthusiasm and motivation about participation—those whose direct supervisors participated alongside them on a daily basis.

This also aligned with my research that leaders can nurture self-efficacy, reinforce collective efficacy, and encourage engagement by creating a positive team environment that encourages commitment to the well-being of the group.

The paragraph above reminds me of the experience I shared with Michael, the lineman who courageously asked me if he could be assessed privately. It was clear he felt emotionally safe to approach me with a request that must have been difficult for him to ask of me. In retrospect, I can now say with confidence that his ability to approach me was facilitated by the relationship I had nurtured with him and others in the organizations I supported.

———————— ·•◆•· ————————

For me, this final chapter is like the bow you place delicately on top of a nicely wrapped gift. It's about Authentic Leadership, the second framework I used to guide my study. Over the years, I have studied several leadership styles, and though there are many great ones available, I have been a fan and practicing believer of this framework. I quickly adopted it, or, better said, *it* adopted *me.* I believe adopting an authentic leadership style is the conduit for transforming human beings and organizations—it has been for me.

My personal journey with authentic leadership began in 2016 when I enrolled in a women's global executive leadership program that is dedicated to the development and empowerment of women leaders, founded by another authentic leadership guru, Dr. Yasmin Davidds. This is where I was introduced to Bill George's books. I had a master's degree in leadership and management, which sparked my desire to continue exploring leadership studies.

Going through this program was an awakening; I had never experienced this type of leadership training. In a nutshell, I describe it as an inward journey. It wasn't solely learning new leadership technical competencies as I had learned before. Instead, it was discovering who *I was* as a leader by discovering my authentic self. Part of this process was to explore and identify my core values and embrace and utilize my life crucibles as the foundation for growth. It is not for the faint-hearted. It's a difficult journey, yet an extremely transformative one—if you put in the work and trust the process. You must be prepared to take an honest look at yourself and how others are impacted by your behavior. The reward is that by the end of the program, you are not the same person who started. I owe this program for igniting my interest in pursuing my doctorate degree.

If you've been bitten by the leadership bug as I have and you've invested your time and energy to become a great leader, I congratulate you and encourage you to keep at it and fight the good fight; it's a journey. The world needs great leaders. I have been fortunate to have had great ones who role-modeled these attributes and paved the way for me to become a leader. For clarification, I'm not minimizing nor discounting completely the tremendously valuable lessons we can take away from poor leaders. I have had my share of them, too, and that would have to be another book. My mindset now is that I feel extremely grateful for my experiences with poor leaders as well because instead of focusing on how poorly they led, I acknowledge that they did the best they could with the tools they had or were given.

To some degree, it's not their fault for being poor leaders. I repeat *to some degree* because there is something called—drum roll please—accountability. The reason I write this is that it's not their fault entirely. I'm convinced recruiting and hiring poor leaders is a systemic issue in many companies and organizations. It's what most of us know because the standard for recruiting, hiring, and promoting leaders has been primarily focused on technical competencies.

Because of this standard, many of us have spent our lives focusing on leadership technical competencies and have overlooked the critical component that emotional intelligence serves in leadership. Another poignant statement made by fellow colleague, Bill Martin, "We have created an imagined reality that those with the highest degrees and the highest grades make the best leaders. A person with the highest grade in music does not necessarily become the best musician."

Authentic Leadership

A concept developed by Bill George, authentic leadership is an approach that emphasizes the essential leader attributes of leading with one's heart, understanding and having passion for one's purpose, being core values-driven, practicing self-discipline, and creating trust-centered relationships. It is about the leader's capacity to lead others guided by these attributes and utilizing them to empower others on their journey.[26] I would

---

[26] George, *True North*, xxxi.

like to add that it's also about serving those on our teams, and specifically for me, it was serving those in the organizations I supported. Bill George has written several leadership books. One of the books, *True North*, is what I refer to as my personal authentic leadership journey guide and can be used simultaneously with his workbook of the same title. Used together, the books help the reader discover their authentic self by taking a journey inward.

Because authentic leaders lead with their hearts, they serve their people with compassion and empathy and make tough decisions from an intuitive and cognitive space. As you learn to evolve into an authentic leader, you learn what your purpose is and lead from *that* space; however, when leaders serve without a passionate purpose, they become susceptible to leading from a place of narcissism because their leadership style is ego-driven. As an authentic leader in training, you get to learn (or revisit) what your core values are, and then you lead from them diligently.

Authentic leaders lead from an integrity lens; consequently, they make decisions from a place of conviction to do the right thing, even if it is difficult. Creating trusting relationships is also an essential mark of an authentic leader. Trust is *the* foundational ingredient for building and sustaining a positive and emotionally safe work environment. My experiences with linemen Michael and Bob served as gentle reminders and proof that fostering trusting relationships is *the* most essential building block for an emotionally safe work environment.

Authentic leaders live a self-disciplined life as well. They understand the importance of the congruence between actions and words, and they model their words with action, aka they "walk the talk." For me, the integrity attribute facilitated self-discipline because I never wanted to sacrifice people's worth and safety for performance or money.

A critical step in becoming an authentic leader is a transformational journey that occurs when leaders embrace various crises in their lives. Bill

George refers to these crises as crucibles, which are essential for becoming an authentic leader.[27]

Crucibles are adversities experienced in life that most often are very painful, yet they can serve as the foundation for growth and change. Leaders can use the power of their crucibles to transform themselves and thus transform organizations. How, you ask? Instead of being victimized by their crucibles, authentic leaders utilize them as a driving force for leading organizations with empathy, compassion, vulnerability, and passion. It's developing gratitude for those painful experiences because, without them, we wouldn't be who we are today.

Correlating Authentic Leadership and Engagement

Proponents and practitioners of the authentic leadership theory believe that to make leaders more effective, one must lead with heart, values, passionate purpose, self-discipline, and relationship, which will equip one to deal with organizational challenges more effectively. Authentic leaders increase employee engagement by building trusting and meaningful relationships. The correlation between authentic leadership, trust, and employee engagement is that employee engagement increases when there is a sound sense of trust between employee and leader.

Leaders who adopt authentic leadership not only support their employees but also demonstrate a deep commitment to them. The result is they build enduring relationships, which, in turn, increases employee engagement. Fostering an organizational culture that focuses on building enduring relationships requires leaders to be integrity-driven in their actions and demonstrate self-discipline while living out those actions to meet the needs of their employees.

---

[27] George, *True North*, 45.

Because of the emotional intelligence foundation of authentic leadership theory, authentic leaders learn how their behavior impacts people, and consequently, they can rally employees toward a common vision. One case study I found showed that 386 workers from 1,500 Taiwanese service and manufacturing companies who trusted their leaders were more positively engaged.[28] Trust was the basis of meaningful relationships between leader and employee, which confirmed that a mutually reinforcing relationship between trust and work engagement exists. Another study on employee engagement resulting from authentic leadership involved 391 workers from a variety of industries in the United States. These study findings showed that employee engagement was a byproduct of authentic leadership.[29]

Interviews with the Linemen

As I mentioned in previous chapters, I conducted a qualitative study where I interviewed linemen from five separate locations who participated in the organization's injury-prevention program. They also had the lowest participation rate and suffered 80 percent of the company's sprain and strain injuries. Their responses were going to answer my third research question, designed to explore participant perception of their immediate supervisor's leadership attributes. Specifically, I posited whether supervisors exemplified any authentic leadership attributes that influenced their participation in the program.

At the conclusion of all the interviews, four meaningful themes were revealed related to authentic leadership attributes that influenced their

---

[28] Dan-Shang Wang, & Hsieh, Chia-Chun, "The Effect of Authentic Leadership on Employee Trust and Employee Engagement," *Social Behavior and Personality* 41, no. 4 (2013): 613-624. https://doi.org/10.2224/sbp.2013.41.4.613.

[29] Hua Jiang & Luo, Yi, "Crafting Employee Trust: From Authenticity, Transparency to Engagement," *Journal of Communication Management* 22, no. 2 (2018): 138–160, https://doi.org/10.1108/JCOM-07-2016-0055.

participation: 1) supervisors encouraged work behavior showing integrity, 2) supervisors extended compassion during COVID-19, 3) supervisors encouraged and facilitated professional work relationships, and 4) supervisors failed to model program participation. We will dive into these authentic leadership attributes in more detail in the next chapter.

Chapter Takeaways

- Create an environment that is emotionally safe for employees to speak up without fear of reprisal.
- Ensure that there are standards or mandates in place for recruiting, hiring, and promoting leaders who possess technical expertise and competencies AND who lead from a place of awareness, vulnerability, and authenticity.
- Be a leader who acknowledges, understands, and embraces the positive power of your crucibles. Your crucibles have the power to transform you and your organization.

Focus Questions

- What connections have you made about your leadership style and its impact on those you lead?
- What are you doing to foster an environment for your employees to freely share their organizational concerns?
- What processes and procedures does your organization have in place to recruit, hire, and promote candidates who have the relational skills and competencies for building trusting relationships with employees?

CHAPTER 6

SNAPSHOTS OF AUTHENTIC LEADERSHIP

Bill George stated, "Above all, leadership is a human undertaking. When leaders reveal their vulnerabilities, they develop trusting human connections with others that motivate and empower those they engage."[30] This quote leads me to share a few more experiences I had with four leaders in the utility company: Sean, Avery, Pablo, and Dr. Helbourne.

In the next chapter, you will read about my experience with Andy, so I'll share about Sean first because the two are interconnected. Sean was the hiring manager for the safety position I interviewed for originally,

____

[30] George, *True North*, 82.

and both Sean and Andy were part of my interview panel. During the interview, which Sean led, he had a poker face that was very unnerving. Immediately, I noticed he was straightforward, concise, and had an overall no-nonsense approach. The interview went well, and, as you know, I got the job.

I was excited and grateful for the opportunity to begin my safety career journey and support a mix of field and office workforce despite my "non-traditional" status. ("Traditional" was a commonly used term for people who worked in the organization and had a lineman-work background. Being a traditional in this organization meant you had "street cred.") Sean and Andy shared similar characteristics. Sean was also a former lineman who worked his way up the ranks in the field and eventually into safety leadership. I was spot-on regarding what I'd picked up intuitively about Sean during my interview. He, too, had a big presence and, in true lineman form, had no problem being blunt. From the start, Sean was extremely forthright about his expectations of me. He made it crystal clear that there was only one thing that would make him angry and something I should never do. I'll never forget when he drove me to my office so I could get acquainted with everyone. He said:

> *You need to know that there is something that will make me extremely angry, and that is tardiness. If you are fifteen minutes early to a meeting, in my book, you're late. I expect you to be at every meeting at least thirty minutes before the start time.*

I etched those words on the forefront of my brain and held to them. Sean intimidated me on many levels because, along with his mastery of the "poker face," he was somewhat aloof, wicked smart, and had a dry sense of humor. I felt like I could never read him.

On the other hand, his leadership style surprised me somewhat; it was dichotomous. He was very verbal and reassured me often that I was doing a good job; he didn't micromanage me, and he always welcomed my opinion. When I made mistakes, he was not judgmental. Instead, he'd asked me what my lesson was and how I planned to do it differently next time. Sean was also a taskmaster, which helped me with time management. He had me fill out a weekly project track sheet so he could keep abreast of what I was working on, which we discussed on our weekly calls. He was very diligent with his employees obtaining the necessary training to be successful safety professionals. He sent me to several training courses so I could understand the nature of outside construction crew work. I learned so much from him.

Overall, we had a harmonious working relationship. That changed, however, one early afternoon while I was driving back from conducting a crew visit. Sean called to check in on me, as he usually would. I let him know that I had conducted a crew visit but decided to get an early start on the freeway heading home since I was almost three hours away. Immediately, Sean became angry, raised his voice, and began to scold me. He fired off rapidly that if I didn't have enough work, he had work for me to do and named all the projects that I *could be* working on since I wasn't "busy enough" with my current workload. I couldn't get in *one word* during his rant. I became nervous and upset and decided the best thing to do was to remain quiet and exit the freeway. I can't recall how the call ended; however, I do remember thinking how I needed to address what had transpired ASAP. That's exactly what I did. I waited a day or so, then emailed him to let him know that I needed to meet with him. I picked a neutral location and scheduled a conference room. I scripted everything I was going to say and rehearsed it. I was extremely nervous, to say the least.

In summary, when he arrived, I positioned myself directly in front of him and began with, "I asked you to meet me so we can discuss what happened the other day while I was driving." With my voice quivering slightly, I asked him if he was happy with my work thus far and if I had demonstrated that I could be trusted to work autonomously. He responded with a resounding yes. So my next question was, "Then how do you explain your behavior on the phone the other day?" I let him know that I needed to understand what happened that prompted him to behave in such a manner because the way he treated me left me feeling berated and disrespected and that I could not flourish under those conditions.

Sean listened to me so intently that I couldn't predict how he would respond; he surprised me again. His response is what cemented for me that he was truly on a journey and committed to becoming a better leader. He thanked me for bringing it to his attention, validated my feelings, apologized for his behavior, and vowed for it not to happen again; and it never did. A principal belief of authentic leadership is that leaders must be aware of how they lead and the impact on those they lead, and Sean role-modeled that. Our working relationship became better and better over time, and to this day, I consider Sean to be one of the best leaders I've had the pleasure of working with at that company.

Another revealing leadership experience was with Avery. When I met Avery, he had just taken on the role of director in our safety organization. I best describe him in these few words: an authentic and genuine person who was a consummate professional and supporter. Rumor around the office water cooler was that upon arriving at the office, Avery would stop by employees' cubicles to greet and engage them in chat.

Since my office was in another location, I had never experienced that; however, it wasn't long before I had the opportunity to get acquainted with Avery firsthand. The water cooler rumors were true. Avery was engaging and truly wanted to get to know us as human beings. He was sincerely open to feedback about what we liked and didn't like about our organization and encouraged suggestions on how to improve our culture.

Avery was also an advocate of equity for women in the organization and backed it up with his actions. He had a "yes you can" attitude and was committed to championing his female staff to apply for leadership positions that traditionally were held by men. Avery believed in me more than I believed in myself at times. He encouraged me to "spread my wings and fly," meaning he knew I could achieve more and that I should go for it. To this day, he continues to advocate and support me. Avery attended my doctoral graduation ceremony, and, to this day, I consider him an inspirational leader and friend.

Another incredible leadership experience was with Pablo. My working relationship with Pablo began during my fitness career at the company, prior to safety. I met him through a mutual connection. Since Pablo was an avid running aficionado and I was working at the corporate fitness center during that time, our conversations were centered around fitness. Pablo was kind, humble, genuine, approachable, and dynamic.

When I began to pursue a safety career and submitted my résumé for the safety position, I discovered that he was the VP of that organization. Once I was chosen to interview for the position, I emailed him to see if we could meet with the purpose of learning more about the organization. He responded immediately and was very honest that though he was the VP, I would gain more insight by speaking with the organization's director. I was impressed with his humility and honesty. He sent me the director's name and encouraged me to contact him, and I did. Unfortunately, I was informed that this director would be on the interview panel if I reached the final interview stage. This would create an ethical conflict, and as soon as I communicated this to Pablo, he agreed to speak with me. I was deeply impressed with Pablo's desire to help me prepare for the interview. We met a week later, and his insight and words of encouragement inspired me to pursue my safety career and more.

Flash-forward ten years later, Pablo became the CEO of this company, yet his humility and genuineness remained constant. Whenever I saw him in a meeting, he approached me to say hello and asked how I was doing, regardless of his "bigwig" entourage. He always responded to my emails in a timely manner, and once I shared that I was pursuing my doctoral degree, he congratulated me, saying he knew I could do it. He offered continued support. Somewhere along the way, someone shared with me that he had a "doctor" title before his name, yet he never shared that with me. This was another example of his humility.

My most impressionable moment with Pablo was when he discovered that I was leaving the company. He made the time to email and congratulate me; however, he also candidly expressed that he was a bit shocked and wanted to meet with me to understand why. He rearranged his schedule *just* so we could meet virtually. During our meeting, he was just as kind, humble, genuine, approachable, and dynamic as when we first met. To this day, our relationship continues, and so does his advocacy for my success.

Speaking of inspirational leaders, I would be remiss not to mention my experience with Dr. Helbourne (Dr. H). In retrospect, I owe Dr. H for my career with this utility company. When I was hired to work in her corporate medical organization as a health and fitness contractor, she was the company medical director. I'll never forget when I first met her. She was highly intelligent, genuine, energetic, quick-witted, brilliant, and hilariously funny.

Despite her brilliance, she was approachable, down-to-earth, and inclusive. I realized quickly how great of a leader she was. We all had exercise-related degrees. She valued us, treated us with the utmost respect, and gave us the autonomy to be professionals in our field. She was also very intentional about engaging all of us in projects. Because of Dr. H's leadership, we felt that we were contributing to and part of the bigger vision of the company and organization. She was extremely practical in her approach to solving organizational problems and had the uncanny ability to remain objective despite her personal opinions. I spent quite a few years working in her organization and enjoyed it thoroughly. I watched her closely, listened, and learned from her.

Approximately three or so years into my career in the corporate fitness center, there was downsizing and restructuring of departments within that organization. As a result, we had to reinterview for our positions to become permanent company employees. I was fortunate enough to procure a part-time position there, which I gladly accepted. It wasn't long, however, before I had to begin a job search for full-time employment.

Within a month after searching, I was offered a promising career with another company. I was torn because I had envisioned a long-term career with this utility company, and I didn't want to leave. I decided to share with Dr. H. She had created a safe space for us to speak to her openly, so I took the opportunity and let her know that I felt forced to leave a job and company that I loved so much. I asked if there was any possibility of a future opening because if there was, I would hang in there.

She heard me and immediately said, "Well, I most certainly will not lose you. Please let the other company know you'll need a few days to respond." Within forty-eight hours, Dr. H had moved mountains. She had taken this up to the organization's executive leadership team and made a case for me, and they agreed to create a full-time position for me. She called me at home and offered me the job. I cried and cried. I had never felt so valued by a leader as I did with her.

After years of working full-time in that capacity and various conversations later, I shared with her that I was considering a safety career. Of course, as the quintessential advocate she was, she volunteered for me to serve as the safety representative for our department so I could gain safety experience. A couple of years went by, and I was pursuing several safety positions. Once I was chosen for the safety position that Sean hired me for, Dr. H wrote me the most fabulous letter of recommendation; the rest is history.

Years later, Dr. H took an early retirement. I attended her retirement party and asked her, "Why are you leaving?" She responded with what I call now a "golden nugget" of advice. She said, "Sometimes the juice isn't worth the squeeze." Though I laughed at first, later, her words pierced me. What I interpreted from them was that life is so short that sometimes we must walk away. Since then, I have applied this mindset and belief system to many things in my life, both professionally and personally.

There is a definite common thread between my wonderful experiences with the leaders I've written about. They had a relentless commitment to fostering and sustaining trust and connection, they were authentic, approachable, humble, vulnerable, unwavering advocates, and they deeply cared for my well-being and for those they led. Because of their leadership attributes, I was inspired to pursue my goals. I began my doctoral dissertation acknowledgments section with "It takes a village." I am grateful for the leaders in this company who became and continue to be part of my village of supporters and advocates.

Chapter Takeaways

- Be intentional about leading from a place that inspires and motivates your employees to be humble and vulnerable.
- Be relentlessly committed to fostering trusting connections with your employees.

Focus Question

- What actionable steps will you take to reflect on your leadership style to ensure you are leading and role modeling from a place of humility and vulnerability?
- How will you intentionally stay committed to fostering trusting relationships with your employees?

CHAPTER 7

THEMES OF AUTHENTIC LEADERSHIP

One poignant leadership experience that has stayed with me involved former company CEO Carl—a very tall, smart, and quick-witted man who carried himself with utmost confidence. Carl was another leader, like Andy, who I believe was not aware of how his positionality impacted the company employees. Positionality, in a nutshell, can be defined as the way in which a person views themselves and how they impact others. My husband, CP, is a union business manager who collaborates very frequently with all levels of leadership and, more specifically, the executive leadership team. He and Carl established a great working relationship early on.

As a union manager's spouse, I usually attend functions where the company leadership is invited and, thus, I interact with them as well. One year, Carl attended the union Christmas party, and CP asked me to accompany him to greet Carl. I remember my knee-jerk-style reaction was to cringe and say, "Oh no, not Carl." CP was very surprised at my reaction because I was a safety professional in Carl's organization, and he was aware that I had met Carl before, so he curiously asked me why. I responded that though I had many brief encounters at various safety meetings with Carl, many of us felt intimidated by his presence. I also explained to CP that Carl was not aware of his impact on employees. Carl had no idea that his aloofness was intimidating. It's called being unaware of one's positionality, and I will discuss it in the next few paragraphs.

To my shock, the next time CP met Carl for a business dinner, he mentioned my reaction to Carl at the Christmas party, to which Carl reacted very surprised and asked, "How can that be? I'm just Carl." That became our inside joke, so whenever I'd see Carl, I'd say, "Oh look, there's just Carl." The reality is that once I did speak with Carl, we had a pleasant conversation, and I learned that, indeed, he *was* "just Carl." After my conversation with Carl, I had an epiphany that though I had a birds-eye view and constant exposure to the executive leadership team, I was not immune to what others in the company felt and their reaction to interacting with the executive leadership team. This confirmed my thoughts and research about the importance of leaders connecting with their employees.

Just as a restaurant menu features a plethora of food choices, this organization had a menu of leaders with their unique flavors. In my twenty-year career with this utility company, I encountered incredible leaders who connected with their employees and created an emotionally safe work environment, and sometimes I encountered those who didn't. There were some who had a command-and-control style, and it was clear they were not to be questioned—the "do as I say, sir, yes sir" type. Others were collaborative. They had a genuine interest in involving their employees in decision-making to improve work processes, especially as it related to introducing new field crew work protocols and equipment.

Many leaders had the best intentions to connect with their teams and their employees' best interests at heart; however, a disconnect often still existed. I attribute part of the inability to connect with one's employees to positionality, which I defined earlier. Positionality can be from a lens of status, race, gender, class, or sexuality.

Usually, our lens dictates how we interact with others and the choices we make; unfortunately, sometimes our lens clouds perspective. More often than not, in my experience with leaders, this clouded perspective was subconscious. I discovered over the years with this company that most leaders were not aware of their positionality yet scratched their heads, wondering why they weren't connecting with their employees.

As I introduced in Chapter 5, I discovered four meaningful themes related to authentic leadership attributes that influenced employee participation in injury prevention programs across the board—integrity-filled work behavior, compassion, professional work relationships, and supervisors who failed to model program participation.

> *The values of authentic leaders are shaped by their personal beliefs and developed through introspection, consultation with others, and years of experience. The test of authentic leaders' values is not what they say but how they act under pressure. If leaders aren't true to the values they profess, the trust is broken and not easily regained.*[31]

> —*Bill George*

The first theme that I discovered was that their supervisors encouraged them to work with integrity. Sixty-eight percent of the linemen shared that when they experienced conflicts with peers, their immediate supervisors counseled and encouraged values-driven and self-disciplined

---

[31] George, *True North*, xxxii.

behavior—specifically, relationship dynamics pertaining to conflict resolution without sacrificing their integrity. As a result of the supervisors' counseling, the linemen reported that when they treated their peers with integrity and self-discipline under stressful circumstances, the relationships improved, and conflicts were resolved.

The linemen I interviewed—who struggled with their peers—chose to emulate their supervisors, who modeled integrity-driven behavior, and that created a domino-style effect of integrity. The linemen and their peers' relationships improved as a result. How exciting is that? This is a perfect example that leaders' actions indeed influence their employees. Their responses are another excellent example of the outcome when leaders build and foster an organizational culture that focuses on developing enduring relationships with integrity and self-discipline.

In contrast to the linemen's supervisors above, one participant specifically expressed that despite the professional work relationship, he experienced his supervisor as someone who was disconnected from what it took to conduct the work with adequate resources, which consequently impacted the relationship negatively. I had a similar experience with a director of one of the organizations I supported, Kim. Our relationship didn't suffer a negative outcome; however, it was evident that she struggled to connect with the crews.

Kim was wicked smart, funny, energetic, integrity-led, and wanted nothing more for her organization than to keep everyone safe. Kim and I quickly developed a genuine relationship. She created the space for us to speak candidly, and she was sincere in her commitment to support my safety efforts for her organization. We spoke often and met at least once a month so I could keep her abreast of safety issues. Much like me, Kim was not a "traditional." In this culture, the implications and assumptions of being "non-traditional" were that we couldn't conduct our jobs effectively because we had never done utility linemen work.

I felt compassion and empathy for Kim because rumor had it that some employees didn't understand how someone who had never done their work would oversee the organization. This was just like I had experienced. When I was hired as a safety advisor in this organization, I encountered rough times, primarily for the reason I stated above: I wasn't a "traditional." I didn't come from the field and move my way up the ranks to safety.

In fact, I was told by some leaders (and line guys who I supported) that I wouldn't succeed, that I didn't know S#*!, and that I wasn't their first choice as a candidate for the job; however, that didn't stop me. I *knew* I could do the job, be successful, and, most of all, that I could bring value to the organization and keep employees safe. I asked a ton of questions and conducted crew visits at all hours, including middle-of-the-night, so I could learn the work. I wore my PPE and attended all mandated training; I even learned to climb the utility poles.

I'll never forget that sometime before I left the company, one of my safety coworkers, who had been a lineman prior to his safety career, confessed that early on, he had doubts about me doing this work successfully; however, when he saw me at the training yard climbing poles for testing new climbing equipment with my full gear on—including pole gaffs, leather gloves, hard hat, and utility ropes and harness—he said I gained his respect. He was impressed by the ease with which I climbed, and he was shocked that I enjoyed it. He also gave me "kudos" for surviving the disapproval and taunting. I was thrilled with his compliments, thanked him, and let him know that although it had been rough, my thick-skin survival tactics were the result of having two older brothers. Just as older brothers tend to do when one is the youngest and only girl, they torture you for their pure joy and entertainment.

When I found out that some employees were not too thrilled with Kim as the new director, I kept my experiences of being taunted and doubted, both as a young girl and in this position, at the forefront of my mind. These experiences helped me empathize with her. I think our non-traditional status bonded us. Additionally, we were of like-minded spirit, sharing the same passion for safety, and believed that passion would override preconceptions of being non-traditional.

A couple of years later, after Kim started working there, an employee in her organization passed away from an apparent suicide. This news devastated everyone, and people were in shock and disbelief. As expected, Kim and her leadership team followed the safety and security protocols. They arranged with human resources to send grief counseling professionals to the work location. There were many rough moments in that organization after this tragedy, and there was an immense wave of sadness felt each time I visited that location.

Shortly after the employee's death, some employees approached me with concern that when Kim visited them shortly after the tragic news was shared, she had come across as somewhat cold and lacking emotions . . . just aloof overall. She had developed the reputation of being somewhat dry and not a "people person," and this tragedy confirmed it—in their opinion. I knew she didn't lack emotions because I had witnessed, on many occasions, where she demonstrated gigantic emotional gestures, especially when one of her employees was hurt. When she visited the work locations, conducted crew visits, and attended monthly safety meetings, she tried to connect with her employees.

I was also aware that Kim's leadership style was very direct and stern, which was easily interpreted as lacking emotion. In Kim's defense, it wasn't the first time I had encountered women leaders in this organization struggling with finding acceptance and respect while breaking barriers and navigating between the organizational culture, their inherent personalities, and their leadership style and expectations. I often wondered if how

Kim was perceived wouldn't have mattered if she was a male. There were plenty of male leaders in that organization who were direct and aloof, yet they were accepted without complaint.

During one of my one-on-one meetings with Kim, we talked about the aftermath of the tragedy, and she asked how people in her organization were feeling after the employee's death. I appreciated that she truly wanted to know how her people felt. Because of the nature of our relationship, I took a chance and shared with her that some employees had approached me, concerned about her perceived lack of emotion about the employee's death. I added that perhaps she should have been more vulnerable with her emotions because it would have helped connect with them more and changed their perception of her.

What ensued shook me a bit. Kim began to cry and became very agitated. Very powerfully, she slapped her hand on the desk and said, "G*# dammit, Maria, I can't do that; it's all I can give. I must remain strong and cannot let them see me crumble. I have an organization of people to lead, help, and worry about."

My response was, "And this is exactly *why* you should have allowed them to see that you hurt just as they hurt." We went back and forth for a few minutes and agreed to disagree. As disappointed as I was that she held steadfastly to her "why," I realized that perhaps she saw vulnerability as a weakness. Then, I reminded myself that each leader has their own style and that I needed to meet each one where they were with empathy and grace.

I know for certain that Kim gained her line guys' respect for her effort to provide them with the equipment and improved work processes to keep them safe while working. There is no doubt her heart was in the right place because she was a leader who worked with integrity and passion for safety; unfortunately, there was still a disconnect between her and the line guys with respect to building relationships. Their perception was that she was guarded, and perhaps that was a barrier to establishing more connection with her employees.

> As leaders, it is our obligation to work on developing all of the authentic leadership attributes . . . each ones serves its purpose of creating and sustaining a culture of unity, trust, and, consequently, transformation.

Integrity was one of Kim's best leadership attributes. Is being a leader with integrity important? Absolutely, it is; however, it is not the only attribute that will inspire others to change. It is my opinion that, as leaders, it is our obligation to work on developing *all* of the authentic leadership attributes. The way I view leading from a space of authentic leadership is that the five attributes serve as a holistic approach to leading organizations. One attribute builds on the next one, and each one serves its purpose of creating and sustaining a culture of community, unity, trust, and, consequently, transformation.

> *Can you lead authentically without compassion? Not really, although some leaders behave as though they have no compassion for anyone. It is your life experiences that open up your heart to have compassion for the most difficult challenges that people face along life's journey.*[32]
>
> *—Bill George*

---

[32] Bill George, *Authentic Leadership: Rediscovering the Secrets to Creating Lasting Value* (New Jersey: Wiley, 2003), 39.

Everyone endures challenges in their lifetime that impact their performance at work and their home life. As leaders, we must practice compassion with our employees because, chances are, we, too, have encountered challenges. Just as soil is the essential nutrient for a plant to grow, compassion can serve as the soil for growing trust. Trust is a fundamental ingredient that enables leaders to rally those they serve toward a common vision. In my career as a safety professional, and in all my careers, being a compassionate leader set the tone for me to establish and sustain meaningful relationships. In retrospect, the trust that I fostered with the line crews during my career as their safety support was the conduit for their candid responses during the interviews.

> Trust is a fundamental ingredient that enables leaders to rally those they serve toward a common vision.

When I asked the linemen to describe a time when their direct supervisor demonstrated an act of kindness, six linemen shared that their supervisors expressed and demonstrated gratitude and appreciation toward them for their daily work during the difficult pandemic times. They also shared that their supervisors demonstrated kindness and compassion by taking a genuine interest in their well-being (and their families) by extending a helping hand, such as delivering food to them and accommodating their work schedules to meet the employees' and families' needs. Their responses validated the literature I found about authentic leaders who practice compassion and empathy. In the linemen's eyes, their supervisors leading with their hearts and taking a genuine interest in them made a difference to them.

> *Enduring relationships are built on connectedness and a shared purpose of working toward a common goal.*[33]
>
> —*Bill George*

I shared the previous story about Kim's genuine effort to connect with her field crews to show that, though her heart was in the right place because of her dedication to the safety of all employees in her organization, a relational disconnect still existed between Kim and the line guys. This disconnection led to the crews' perception that she was difficult to get to know, and they viewed her as insincere. Though my personal experience with Kim was that she was sincere, the crews' perspective wasn't, unfortunately. I understood them because, in too many work environments, any aloofness is mistaken for being disingenuous, and vulnerability is mistaken as a weakness. As I quoted Bill George above, "When leaders take a risk, shed the hard exterior, and allow themselves to be vulnerable, *that* is the opportunity to foster deep connected relationships."

I asked the linemen to share how they would describe their relationship with their immediate supervisor, and six linemen shared with me that there was a personal component to the relationship they experienced. They categorized their relationships with their supervisors in various ways, such as mentors who led by example and even referred to them as friends—friends who had earned their fond respect. Three of the linemen categorized their work relationship with their supervisors as both professional yet complicated because they perceived that a supervisory disconnect existed about the work and what it took to get the work done. They emphasized feeling unsupported regarding the allocation of resources and personnel needed to conduct work safely and effectively.

There was a common thread between the linemen's relationship experiences with their supervisors and the authentic leadership theory

---

[33] George, *Authentic Leadership*, 40.

literature I explored. The literature stated that authentic leaders can rally their employees toward a shared vision when they support and are committed to their employees because of building trusting and enduring relationships that foster connection. A principal belief of authentic leadership is that leaders must be aware of how they lead and the impact on those they lead, which I touched on with positionality. Additionally, it is critical for leaders to demonstrate vulnerability without thinking that doing so is a sign of weakness. This leads me to my next leadership experience, Andy. I have *so* many experiences with Andy that they could easily become another book.

Andy was the "head honcho" of the field operations of the organization I first supported and was linemen Bob and Michael's manager (three levels higher, to be exact). I first met Andy when I interviewed for the safety position in his organization; he was on the interview panel along with Sean, who I mentioned in the previous chapter. Truth be told, Andy made me nervous because he was a big man, not only in stature but in his presence, voice, and personality. He made piercing, direct contact with my eyes as he asked me the questions. I got through it, was so happy when the interview concluded, and, hey, I got the job!

Andy had worked for the company for nearly forty years when I started my safety position. He was a former lineman who worked his way up the ranks, so his knowledge of the trade was solid. As I wrote above, Andy's personality was BIG, and he made his presence known. Andy's leadership style was as big as his presence; he was the epitome of a command-control hierarchy. It wasn't long before I noticed the impact of Andy's personality and leadership style on the relational dynamics in that organization. He had developed the reputation of being tough-minded, stubborn, and inflexible.

It is my opinion that Andy was a *tad* extra hard on the linemen than he was on the office staff; I attributed this to his low tolerance of unsafe practices in the field. During the many years of his lineman career, he had witnessed life-altering accidents and a few fatalities, so I understood and respected that. Though Andy never demonstrated any sign of vulnerability, as I got to know him, I learned that there was a soft side to him that he kept tucked and hidden from many. I felt fortunate and honored that he began to "let me in." I know in my heart that Andy meant well—he really did and didn't want anyone hurt—however, he was *oblivious* to his positionality and how that impacted his line guys.

I continued forging ahead, leading from my authenticity—from my heart and values and with passion for all employees' safety. As a result, as time passed, the linemen became very comfortable with me and began to share about the multiple safety protocols and procedures that needed to change. They also shared their concern about outdated equipment because they were potential safety hazards. Since I was new and unfamiliar with how they conducted their work, I relied on my crew visits to watch and learn, as well as on his leadership team and mine. I had questions *all* the time, and they were proud and excited to share their knowledge with me.

I was able to convince Bob, Michael, and a few others to join the safety team because they were experienced linemen, knew their trade well, and, most of all, they were bold. I knew I could count on them to inform me about the safety equipment they needed. I met with the safety team monthly, which was usually a couple of weeks before the monthly organizational safety meeting that all employees and leadership attended.

After a few months of meetings (both with the team and the organization), I picked up on another culture trend. For every idea or request made by the line guys at the safety meetings, Andy blasted his "ready, aim, fire" approach. Often, he'd shut down an idea, especially when it came to new equipment requests. I noticed how defeated the safety team members became after the monthly organization meetings. They'd immediately bombard me with "this culture will *never* change" comments. It got to the point that the safety team didn't want to speak or request anything if Andy was present at the meetings, especially when he stood in front of the assembly room. It was very discouraging, to say the least, and I felt that we were not going to move in the needed direction if this continued. I asked the team to trust me and that I would "handle Andy."

In a private meeting between Andy and me, I asked him if he was aware of how he came across in the meetings and how he was perceived by the guys—he said he wasn't aware. I informed him cautiously that the crews felt defeated and believed their requests weren't being heard.

He was adamant in attempting to convince me that the guys were only asking for new equipment because they wanted "shiny new toys." I was taken aback by this because, based on what I was learning from the crew visits, asking my field leadership, and comparing equipment from other fieldwork locations, new equipment and tools were needed desperately. I disagreed graciously and let him know that, indeed, there was a need for upgraded tools and equipment because I had inquired with my safety leadership and other resources.

When I expressed a different opinion than his, it didn't go over well. He was glaring at me with disapproval and added that I only cared for what line guys wanted. I reassured him that I was there to serve everyone in the organization, *including* him. Andy also shared that he didn't appreciate being blindsided by their requests. He had a budget to consider, so he couldn't say yes to everything they wanted. I had another "aha" moment. I never considered that he felt caught off-guard at each meeting, and I failed to take the budget into consideration. I thanked, acknowledged, and validated him.

It was great feedback, and our one-on-one ended well. I asked if he was interested in meeting with me prior to the safety meetings so I could give him a heads-up, and this way, he wouldn't feel blindsided. He agreed. My suggestion to meet prior to all meetings helped solidify our relationship.

From that moment on, I knew I could ask him anything, whether it was uncomfortable or not, and he was very okay with speaking with me candidly.

Flash-forward to all subsequent meetings. The briefing prior to each organization's safety meeting became Andy and my ritual. We were quite the comedy act—sort of the Andy and Maria show. It started first thing in the morning. He'd see me, *walking-with-a-purpose* toward his office with my folders in hand. We'd greet each other with a pleasant "good morning," then he'd look down while shaking his head no and muttering, "Ay que la," which translates to "Oh, what the." It was his funny way of expressing concern for *whatever* I was about to bring up. Once in his office, I'd wait for him to sit back (comfortably) in his chair. Then I'd lean into his desk and ask, "Did you take your blood pressure medicine, Andy? If not, please do so now." He'd chuckle, and then we'd proceed with our pre-meeting briefing.

After a few pre-meeting briefings with Andy, I took another courageous chance and asked Andy to stand in the back of the assembly room once the safety meeting started instead of his usual front and center; of course, I explained why it was important for him to do so. Remember I mentioned a few paragraphs above: "It got to the point that the safety team didn't want to speak or request anything if Andy was present at the meetings, especially when he stood in front of the assembly room." Additionally, I was able to convince him to refrain from interrupting while anyone spoke. I recall on various occasions when Andy's nonverbal gestures spoke louder than his verbal ones—his deep breaths and his fidgeting—but all I had to do was look at him, connect eyes, and he'd stop. That's all it took. Like magic!! These were HUGE steps for Andy, and I'm so grateful he obliged me for the sake of his organization.

Though I struggled occasionally over the years with Andy, I don't regret one moment. It was a valuable learning lesson for me. Every day I had to be intentional about practicing empathy, grace, patience, and bottom line, I had to meet him where he was. Andy and I grew closer as a result, and when he retired, he invited me to his retirement party. I was honored.

⋅⋅◆◆◆◆⋅⋅

Kim, Andy, and Carl are classic examples of leaders who believed they genuinely had the best intentions and their employees' best interests at heart. Despite their intentions, however, a disconnect still existed. Effective leaders must acknowledge and then intentionally work on understanding their positionality and its impact.

Increasing our awareness of how others view us will increase our capacity for understanding, compassion, grace, and empathy for others, which will foster stronger and more trusting relationships with employees. This leads me to the next two leadership experiences I encountered.

After Andy retired, his successor, Tommy, was the manager who was second in command during Andy's reign. It was a very easy transition once he took over. Tommy had a deep desire to take care of his people, and his goal was to make his organization a safe place to work, both physically and psychologically. He was genuine, very approachable, an out-of-the-box thinker, and listened intently when his employees expressed any concerns.

I was impressed with how Tommy would begin his day every day. Shortly after arriving in the office, he'd walk up and down the corridors of the cubicles in the entire building section. He would greet everyone and ask how they were doing or ask about their families. Sometimes, he'd spend a little more time in a person's cubicle, depending on their conversation, and it was clear that everyone appreciated his effort to get to know them. I believe his morning ritual was the foundation for the employees' ease around Tommy; they felt valued, respected, included, and appreciated. He showed he cared.

Safety meetings were always pleasant with Tommy as the leader. At every meeting, he allowed the employees to lead because he wanted to hear them before he spoke. Once the meetings concluded, Tommy would praise and congratulate everyone for a job well done and remind them that he was there for them. My relationship with Tommy was ideal, and I couldn't have asked for a better leader; it was reciprocal and seamless. He was extremely receptive to any suggestions I made and often approached me for my insight about improving the organization's culture, which also made me feel valued and appreciated. We stayed committed to communicating constantly about what was happening in his organization. We made tremendous strides with safety and the safety culture in the organization because of his leadership. Unfortunately, some years later, he retired as well, and everyone was sorry to see him go.

Another manager whose organization I also supported, Matthew, had a similar leadership style to Tommy. When I began supporting Matthew's organization, I was a bit concerned because I had big shoes to fill, and I was reminded of this from the start. Their former safety specialist did a fantastic job, was very well-liked, and was extremely well-connected with all employees and leadership. I provided the best service I could, keeping their safety at the forefront of my mind and operating from my authentic space.

Matthew made my job easy. He was extremely approachable, humble, genuine, had a sincere desire to keep his people safe, and had a great sense of humor. Everything went smoothly from the start, and my relationship with Matthew and his leadership blossomed. At each organizational safety meeting, I provided the usual safety statistical data, but Matthew was very open to the idea of me facilitating presentations about teamwork and creating a positive safety culture. This was great news for me because I was a year-plus into my doctoral program and was excited for the opportunity to share and practice what I was learning.

A few years later, during a meeting with the safety committee and leadership, the committee members expressed their concern that they had become stagnant and questioned their influence on the organization's employees. This team shared a common vision regarding safety and did great work to ensure organizational safety. The missing link, in my opinion, was they lacked emotional cohesion and trust amongst the team itself. Naturally, I thought, *How can they inspire others and bond at a deeper level when they hadn't done so themselves?* I was confident with what was needed, so I prepared a presentation about how storytelling can influence and inspire trust and engagement. I presented my idea at the next meeting, which was a two-day conference at a beautiful hotel up the coast. It was the perfect setting for a team-building event.

The day of my presentation arrived, and I must admit I was a little anxious because this was definitely an unconventional safety method, especially in this company's culture where soft skills were not prioritized, encouraged, or celebrated as technical expertise was. I kept reminding myself that the bottom line was that we are *all* human with experiences that have shaped and skewed our perspectives and that regardless of our barriers, we all have a subconscious need for belonging and connection.

I was confident it would work. I decided to lead by example and began to share my story. It was well received, and it set the tone for vulnerability as everyone shared, including Matthew, who opened his heart and soul, a true example of unguarded transparency for his employees to witness.

This activity was a true team-bonding experience and one of the most memorable meetings in my safety career. I still miss working with Matthew, his leadership team, and the employees in his organization, but I am happy I have fond memories. When I let Matthew know that I was taking an early retirement from the company to focus on my last year of my doctoral studies, here's what he emailed me:

> *Thank you for everything you did for us. It was you and your creative ways of helping and leading that brought us together. I remember you telling us that to go to the next level, we needed to tell a story. I also remember thinking, "Where is she going with this?" We then told a story, and the rest is history; we became closer and family-like—we owe a lot to you.*

My experiences with Matthew and Tommy serve as proof that when one leads from a place of passion, values, heart, and authenticity, it provides employees with a safe place to express their opinions, creates and sustains trust, and confirms what Bill George stated in the quote that I introduced in this section: "Enduring relationships are built on connectedness and a shared purpose of working toward a common goal."

Another tenet of authentic leadership theory is to be value-driven, consistent, and self-disciplined. What does this look like in real life, however? In simple terms, leaders must practice consistently what they preach, a.k.a., they must "lead by example." Even though some leaders are faced with temptations to behave counter to what they know is best for their employees and organizations, authentic leaders are driven by their conviction to do the right thing and consistently model the behavior they desire to see in their employees; this takes self-discipline. Employees will enthusiastically follow leaders who walk the walk and talk the talk.

When I asked the linemen to describe their immediate supervisor's participation in the program, only two of the nine shared that their supervisors modeled full participation. It was nice to hear that these two shared with enthusiasm in their voices. They added that their supervisors' modeling participation influenced them to continue participation.

Unfortunately, many leaders don't practice self-discipline and follow their words with action. Instead, they set a double standard for themselves and their employees. This was the case for the remaining seven linemen I interviewed. They shared they had witnessed little to zero supervisor participation. Linemen Michael shared, "Since he's been my supervisor, I've never seen him do it." Another lineman, Larry, described his supervisor's participation as, "Yeah, zero. Big fat zero," and described his supervisor's non-participation as "hypocritical." Larry concluded the interview with his view about the importance of supervisors modeling desired behavior about participation. He said, "It is very hypocritical for him to suggest we should participate then not participate himself. It's a problem because he is a leader, and I think it's a role that he should consider if he wants us to participate."

Failing to walk the talk is extremely detrimental to building a culture centered on trust.

Just as these linemen shared with me, I have witnessed many leaders do the same. Failing to "walk the talk" is extremely detrimental to building a culture centered on trust. In fact, some of the research I found named this double standard *corporate hypocrisy.* That is when employees perceive incongruence between the leader's words and actions, which consequently creates barriers to employee engagement. It sets the tone for the perception that the leaders are being hypocritical, as the linemen confirmed.

> *Authentic leaders know competing successfully takes a consistently high level of self-discipline in order to produce results.*[34]
>
> —*Bill George*

---

[34] George, *True North*, xxxiii.

Another lineman, John, shared that COVID-19 influenced his supervisor's participation, but only slightly and then participation dwindled completely:

> *Prior to COVID-19, his participation was about 5 percent. A few times out of the week, I may have seen him participating, but then he would disappear or not participate with the group. He may have participated in the stretches with us occasionally in a meeting or when higher leaders were present. After COVID-19, I think there has been zero participation.*

It is evident by the linemen's responses that most supervisors failed to lead by example. Their responses align with authentic leadership theory research related to leader attributes and their influence on employee participation. The leaders' lack of modeling program participation negatively affected the linemen's participation despite their desire to participate.

Recall this culture's hierarchy and remember that everyone's personality is unique. Some employees had no problem challenging their authority, while others chose not to. Instead, they complied regardless of the outcome. Because of the prioritization of emergent work and the additional organizational barriers discussed in earlier chapters, some linemen felt they could not challenge the leadership hierarchy deeply entrenched in *that* culture. Despite those organizational barriers, overall the linemen were not deterred from participating in the program.

I was pleasantly surprised to hear how the linemen's high value for the program and their equally high self-efficacy levels served as motivators for their continued participation. I can only wonder how much more engagement there would have been if their supervisors had modeled participation.

This chapter also aligns with additional research about employee engagement in worksite health programs, corporate hypocrisy, and failure to link employee health and safety with corporate initiatives.

To achieve 100 percent employee engagement in worksite health and injury-prevention programs, supervisors must be participatory, supportive, and enthusiastic regarding the program. Additionally, when leaders do not exemplify integrity and self-discipline and fail to lead by example, employees lose trust that the company and organization care more for productivity than their health and safety. Leaders must model the behavior they desire to foster and sustain, be passionate about the change effort, and align their goals with those of the organization and company.

Also, there is research that validates the correlation between employee health, productivity, company benefits, and worksite programs. Chronic diseases . . . are the leading causes of death and disability in the United States. They are also leading drivers of the nation's $4.1 trillion in annual healthcare costs.[35] Employees aren't getting the sleep they need, some have poor diets, and they lack physical activity (aside from physical activity at work). These factors put employees at higher risk for work-related accidents, diseases, and increased medical costs.

In chapter two, I wrote that 70 percent of companies provide on-site health prevention programs. Organizations that invest their effort in programs do so because it will benefit the company by a potential 25 percent reduction in medical costs and workers' compensation costs, as well as improve employee health and productivity. Additionally, I shared that less than 50 percent of employees participate in these worksite programs. The research showed that all arrows point to good leadership when it comes to increasing engagement. If leaders participate with enthusiasm, it has

---

[35] "About Chronic Diseases," Centers for Disease Control and Prevention, July 21, 2022, https://www.cdc.gov/chronicdisease/about/index.htm.

a positive influence on their employees, which often results in increased participation.

A *critical* factor in ensuring the positive financial outcomes of worksite programs and increasing engagement is the role of leadership. Leaders at all levels are responsible and must be held accountable for creating and sustaining a culture that supports employee engagement and for aligning and linking employee health and safety to company protocols and processes.

> The research showed that all arrows point to good leadership when it comes to increasing engagement.

Though my job as a safety advisor was to ensure employee physical safety (e.g., has PPE, following safety protocols/procedures, etc.), my mission and passion were to foster a safety culture where all employees felt emotionally safe to speak their voice without reprisal, to hear what they had to say (good, bad, or indifferent), and for them to know I had their best interests at heart.

I attribute my success as a safety professional to leading from a place of authenticity. I diligently practiced what I learned in my journey to become an authentic leader and used my experience with great and not-so-great leaders and growing up with older brothers. The end result was that I fostered relationships built on trust, which enabled me to build a community that focused on a shared vision. Fostering relationships built on trust is the foundation of a flourishing culture. As leaders, aka change agents, we must fight the good fight for our people and listen actively to what employees say, even if we may not agree. Invest time in them and get to know who they are. Care about each one by asking about them, their families, their kids, and what they did on the weekend. Model the behavior you want to see. Be a person of your word. Practice empathy, humility, and transparency (people know when we're not being sincere).

Organizational climates where employees are disengaged, fear retaliation, and lack trust in leadership will not thrive or transform. The alternative rests in authentic leaders who are equipped with social competencies. They build meaningful relationships with their employees, create environments where employees feel emotionally safe to trust, and consequently transform organizations.

Being a leader is easy in theory; however, in practice, it's not as easy for most. It takes intentionality *every day*!! Take it from me—I'm proof; I researched it and lived it.

Chapter Takeaways

- Be vigilant about how your positionality shapes the way you view yourself and how it impacts others (it can be from a lens of status, race, gender, class, or sexuality).
- Data shows that 70 percent of companies provide on-site health prevention programs, and less than 50 percent of employees participate. Be a leader who participates with enthusiasm. Your enthusiasm will be contagious and will be a positive influence on your employees and can result in increased participation.
- Commit to being a courageous leader who prioritizes investing in your company's injury-prevention programs. The result will be a reduction in medical costs and workers' compensation costs, as well as improved employee health and productivity.
- Be a leader who is committed to self-accountability and ownership. Leaders at all levels are responsible and must be held accountable for creating and sustaining a culture that supports employee

engagement, as well as for aligning and linking employee health and safety to company protocols and processes.

Focus Questions

- Do you reflect on how your positionality impacts employees' views of you?
- How does your positionality shape your perspectives?
- What steps are you taking to ensure your organizational leaders are supporting and participating in worksite injury-prevention programs to inspire, motivate, and increase employee participation?
- What accountability processes and procedures are in place for leaders to foster and sustain a culture of engagement?

CONCLUSION

O ver the course of the last seven chapters, I've shared with you the various factors that influenced employee participation in injury-prevention programs—from the organizational obstacles to the motivational factors—and how authentic leadership is the most vital component of engagement.

I've always been a believer that every life experience prepares us for our next endeavor. It is similar to when children play with building blocks, which serves to develop their foundational life skills. Writing this conclusion prompted me to reflect on what building blocks played a role in my leadership genesis. What led me to seek this dissertation topic? Why my passion for building community? Why my passion for safety, health, and wellness? Who were my first leadership models? Where did my relentless drive to improve my life and others' lives come from?

All arrows point to my childhood. I recall when I was approximately eight or nine years old, in the first house we lived in after we emigrated from Ecuador to the United States. The house had an amazingly tall porch, which resembled a stage and overlooked our beautiful front lawn. I loved to rally the neighborhood kids around "the stage" and have discussions about life, put on talent shows, and teach them exercise and dance. I used a "microphone" (my mom's hairbrush) and ensured everyone was well-rehearsed with lines and movements memorized and moved in unison. Clearly, this was the beginning of my passion for building community, safety, and exercise (aka wellness and health).

Who were my first leadership models? Where did my relentless drive to improve my life and others' lives come from? Without a doubt, my parents were my first role models. In Ecuador, my father was a famous musician who made a bountiful living; however, he lacked formal education and knew our lifestyle would be short-lived. He and my mother decided to seek the "American Dream" and move us to the United States. My father immigrated first, then almost two years later, my mother, two brothers, and I followed. He washed dishes at a local restaurant and later worked as a janitor until his retirement at age seventy. My mother worked in housekeeping at a local beach hotel, then as a factory worker until her retirement at age sixty-five.

My father was extremely intuitive and charismatic. He had a gift for sharing his anecdotes that helped him cope with difficult moments in his life. For example, he would say, "I treat people according to their deficiencies." I now interpret this as his relational dynamic mindset. His ability to accept people as they were with compassion, empathy, and without judgment was honorable.

I once read a quote in one of my textbooks by Bolman and Deal, who wrote, "A frame is a coherent set of ideas or beliefs forming a prism or lens that enables you to see and understand more clearly what's going on in the world around you."[36] Both of my parents' combined attributes, such as work ethic, courage, passion, vision, sense of humor, relational skills, empathy, persistence, friendliness, and warmth, were some of the attributes that served as the frame for my life's passion and courage. They worked tremendously hard to give us a life filled with endless opportunities—mission accomplished.

------

[36] Lee G. Bolman and Deal, Terrence, E., *Reframing Organizations: Artistry, Choice, and Leadership* (New Jersey: Wiley, 2017).

Impactful data and compelling linemen's stories are woven throughout these chapters. Data such as, "Every seven seconds, an employee is injured while working because of a sprain and strain injury," and "In 2015, 80 percent of injuries to private industry workers were sprains and strains,[37] and in 2014 they accounted for 25 percent of workers compensation costs, making for an economic burden of $15.1 billion annually."[38] Also, stories like Michael's—remember him? He was the lineman who asked me discreetly if he could be assessed privately because he feared "failing" the vendor's assessment and the negative implications that would follow.

This gripping data I discovered in my journey—and my awareness and understanding of Michael and the linemen who had resigned themselves to painful work for the rest of their lives—reinforced my "why" *exponentially*. This is data that *should* immediately become any leader's "why" to address this injury crisis and motivate them to action.

The other reality that I cannot ignore is that their stories also confirm we have a long and arduous journey ahead of us in recruiting leaders who not only possess strong technical expertise but who can also serve as change agents for transforming a safety culture without sacrificing the integrity of espoused company values.

I invite you to explore and rediscover your "why." We, as leaders, are the missing link for achieving organizational unity, decreasing injuries, increasing engagement, and creating a safety culture where employees feel safe in reporting injuries without fear of reprisal. It is critical for companies to focus on developing courageous leaders who strive to increase their emotional intelligence by attaining the five attributes of authentic leadership. The research supports that organizations with leaders who lead with integrity and heart, passionate purpose, self-discipline, and values can cultivate thriving organizations.

---

[37] USBLS, "Nonfatal Occupational Injuries," 2016.

[38] "Liberty Mutual," *Business Wire*, 2015.

So much precious time is spent on addressing the bottom line—safety protocols, procedures, and injury-prevention programs to transform safety cultures. The *real* solution is creating a safe zone and cultivating engagement, one leader at a time.

ABOUT THE AUTHOR

For over twenty years, Dr. Maria Silva-Palacios has served in many leadership roles in the health, fitness, and safety industries. She is a culture change agent dedicated to fostering trusting relationships with those she encounters. She rallies employees and executive leadership toward a shared vision to transform organizations and communities. She is also a subject-matter expert in office and field ergonomics to ensure client safety and compliance with Cal-OSHA health/safety regulations.

Dr. Silva-Palacios received her doctoral degree in organizational change and leadership from the University of Southern California. She holds a master of science in leadership and management with a concentration in organizational development and human resource management from the University of La Verne and a bachelor's degree in kinesiology with a minor in business management. Additionally, Dr. Silva-Palacios is a certified graduate of the Latina Global Executive Leadership Institute and of the Women in Negotiations (WIN) from UC San Diego Rady School of Executive Development. She also holds a certificate in Environmental/Occupational Health and Safety from California State University, Dominguez Hills Cal-OSHA Institute.

Dr. Silva-Palacios has been a speaker, presenter, and moderator at multiple safety and health and women's empowerment conferences. Her passion for safety, health, and fitness has resulted in creating Dungeon Fitness, a nonprofit organization dedicated to transforming and empowering the lives of people in her community and beyond.